Sales Prospecting

The Ultimate Guide To Finding Highly Likely Prospects You Can Close In One Call.

By Claude Whitacre

©2014 Claude Whitacre
ISBN-13: 978-1494952327
ISBN-10: 1494952327

Special Thanks

Thanks to my young apprentice Hunter Miller for formatting the book and creating the cover.

Of course, thanks to my wife for making my middle age fun, and for editing the book. She did it for free, didn't complain, and did it quick. Thank you, My Dear.

Although everything in this book is tested and proven, I had to learn it somewhere. Most was learned in the field, but there are book authors that have contributed much to my success.
Tom Hopkins, Bill Cates, Bob Burg, Art Sobczak, Bill Good, Paul S. Goldner, Neil Rackham, Jeffrey Gitomer, Zig Ziglar, David Sandler, Alan Weiss, and Oren Klaff. I can't thank them enough. Occasionally, I'll see something in a book, that I use every day. I'll say to myself, "So *that's* where I picked that up!"

My audiences give me great feedback on ideas they have tried, and their results. So, if you're a salesperson, who has heard me speak from the stage. I just want you to know. I enjoyed every minute of it. And thanks for keeping me on my toes.

Special Thanks to Aaron Doud for helping with the title. I'd love to recommend his book but he's too lazy to ever sit down and write it. Hi, Aaron!

As far as terms; I use *customer* and *client* interchangeably. If I say salesman instead of salesperson, forgive me. I write like I talk.

"Have you ever read 'It isn't what you say, it's how you say it'?

Wrong. 'It isn't what you say, or how you say it. *It's who you say it to*'"

-Claude

TABLE OF CONTENTS

Intro 1
Who this book is for. ---------------------------- 1
I'm making a few assumptions here. ---------------- 1
Who it is not for; --------------------------------- 2
I have to get this off my chest ------------------- 3
You still need to sell. ---------------------------- 3

Intro 2
Introduction ------------------------------------- 5
Here's the secret --------------------------------- 6
Why listen to Claude ------------------------------ 7

Chapter 1
The Old Way To Sell, And Why Selling Is Frustrating And Hard. ---------- 9
Why are you taught to cold call? ----------------- 10
Stop Begging For Appointments -------------------- 11

Chapter 2
Call reluctance --------------------------------- 13

Chapter 3
Terrible Prospecting Ideas That Are Still Taught -------------------------- 15
You just aren't making enough calls -------------- 15
3 foot rule. -------------------------------------- 16
Everyone is a prospect ---------------------------- 16
It's a numbers game ------------------------------- 16
Every "No" gets you closer to a "Yes". ---------- 17

Chapter 4
The One Call Closer's Prospecting System ------- 19
Only present to the
"Low Hanging Fruit" ------------------------- 19
These are other situations that
make prospects highly likely to buy ---------------- 20
Sources Of Customers, Best To Worst ------------- 21
Finding high probability prospects.
The turning point in my selling --------------------- 21
Creating A Web Of Buyers Out
Of Highly Probable Prospects ---------------------- 25
Why I recommend You Do
Your Own Prospecting ------------------------------ 26
Is prospecting a separate sales step
from presenting and closing? ----------------------- 27
Scripting Or Going By Ear? ----------------------- 27
Maybe the most important process
that will guarantee success ------------------------- 30
Your warm market. --------------------------------- 33
People you buy from -------------------------------- 35
Selling VS Sorting ---------------------------------- 36

Chapter 5
Cold Calling ----------------------------------- 39
My day getting cold calls --------------------------- 39
First, Cold Calling And
Canvassing? They Work. ---------------------------- 40
Advantages of cold calling -------------------------- 42
Disadvantages of cold calling; ---------------------- 42
A lesson I learned from
a terrible salesperson ------------------------------- 42
Call Reluctance When Cold Calling --------------- 44

*When cold calling, why you only want
to present to the Low Hanging Fruit* --------------- 45
A Cold Calling "Aha" Moment -------------------- 46
The Best Cold Call I Ever Received. --------------- 48
Here's why I loved that cold call; ------------------ 49
*The Secret To Guaranteeing That Your
Cold Calling Is Profitable* -------------------------- 49
*Cold Calling; how much do you
qualify on the phone?* -------------------------------- 50
*Supercharge your results. Add a limitation
that qualifies your best customers.* ----------------- 51
Cold calling scripts; -------------------------------- 53
*If you are calling a business.
Know your contact's name.* ------------------------- 54
*Here's a real life example from my
core business, taken from a transcript.* ------------ 56
*If You Want To Fill Your Day
With Local Appointments.* --------------------------- 62
Objections. Should you handle them? ------------- 64
*If they give you a specific objection
that isn't a stall* -- 67
If you get a "gatekeeper" --------------------------- 68
*If You Have To Cancel An Appointment,
Or If They Postpone It* -------------------------------- 68
Cold Walking --- 69
*The Irresistible Bribe. Prospecting
that creates a feeding frenzy* ------------------------ 69
"I don't want to annoy people" -------------------- 72
*Time waster in the
middle of a cold call* --------------------------------- 73
Sending Direct Mail Before You Call ------------- 75
Call, send, call --------------------------------------- 76
3 call technique -------------------------------------- 77

Why you need other methods of
prospecting besides cold calling ------------------- 78

Chapter 6
Referrals -- **81**
Benefits of referrals; --------------------------------- 81
When I saw the difference between
cold calling and selling by referrals. --------------- 83
Levels of Trust and how
it related to referrals --------------------------------- 86
Seven levels of Trust; Best to worst... -------------- 86
I'd rather have 5 introductions that
referred leads, or a list of 1,000. ------------------- 88
Top sales people work by
referrals, introductions, and
sales to past customers. ------------------------------ 89
Cattle Rustlers VS Ranchers ------------------------ 90
The 80/20 rule in referrals. ------------------------- 91
Should You Get Referrals
From Every Customer? ------------------------------ 93
Why we won't ask for referrals; --------------------- 94
Why people won't give you referrals --------------- 98
They don't want to give you referrals
and introduce you because... ----------------------- 98
Not getting referrals? Here's the
cure; Incredible, proactive service. -------------- 100
The terrible way to ask for referrals,
that you were probably taught...and
why you stopped asking for referrals; ----------- 101
Referring because of you
or because of your offer ---------------------------- 102
Asking everyone for referrals ---------------------- 104
Asking non buyers for referrals -------------------- 104

*Common Objections To
Giving You Referrals* ------------------------------ 105
*The trap of giving you names just
so you'll stop asking.* ------------------------------ 109
*Clients "returning the favor" for
someone who referred them.* ---------------------- 110
*Unsolicited referrals "You
should call my uncle"* ----------------------------- 110

Chapter 7
The One Call Closer's Referral Selling Method ------------------ 113
Your Best Client Profile ---------------------------- 114
Another reason for a Best Client Profile -------- 117
*How I segue into the "Best
Client Profile" discussion* ------------------------- 117
*Preparing the client to welcome and
anticipate the request for referrals* --------------- 117
*The best way to bring up referrals
to get the ball rolling.* ----------------------------- 120
The segue to asking for referrals. ---------------- 120
The power of "By Referral Only" --------------- 121
When to ask for referrals ------------------------- 122
Getting Referrals At The Point Of Sale ---------- 122
*Getting referrals when the client
calls you or needs service* ------------------------- 122
*Getting referrals when the
just gave you a referral.* ------------------------- 123
*Getting referrals right after
you gave them a referral* -------------------------- 123
Not referrals…Introductions ---------------------- 123
Getting the names, and qualifying ---------------- 126
Getting the names --------------------------------- 126

Business sales -------------------------------------- 126
Consumer sales ------------------------------------- 129
Qualifying the referrals as
you receive them. --------------------------------- 131
Qualifying questions to
ask in business sales; ------------------------------ 131
Qualifying questions to ask
in consumer sales: --------------------------------- 134
It's just as easy to get an ideal
referral as a bad one. ------------------------------ 136
Bringing up the idea of introducing
you to the referral. --------------------------------- 137
Here are my results when asking
for the introductions; ------------------------------ 143
Giving results to referrer.
Keep them in the loop. ---------------------------- 144
Referral Incest -------------------------------------- 145
Referral Phone Scripts When
Calling The Referral -------------------------------- 146
Objections to an appointment,
when you call them to set the time. --------------- 147
How to force the meeting in
the next couple of days. ---------------------------- 149
Internet Searches Before
You See The Referral. ------------------------------ 150
When A Referral Counts As A Referral. ---------- 151
E-Mail Introductions; ------------------------------ 151
Researching Your Prospects; --------------------- 153
Voicemail to leave for the prospect -------------- 154
If you have no personal introduction. ------------ 155
Referrals from non-clients ------------------------ 156
Guarantee an avalanche
of qualified referrals ------------------------------- 156

Thanking Referrals And
The Referrer Client -------------------------------- 156
When you get a referral that buys from you ----- 157
When the referral is qualified,
but doesn't buy ------------------------------------ 157
If you get unqualified referrals
that don't buy -------------------------------------- 157

<u>Chapter 8</u>
Past Customers… Your Untapped Vein Of Gold ----------------- 159
You can sell them a new model
of what they have. -------------------------------- 160
You can sell them more of what they have. ------ 161
You can sell them something different. ----------- 161
Company Orphans -------------------------------- 162

<u>Chapter 9</u>
Follow The Salesman -------------------- 165
Warning! --- 170

<u>Chapter 10</u>
What Do They Buy *Before* They Buy *Your* Product/Service? ------------- 173

<u>Chapter 11</u>
Your Elevator Speech ------------------- 179
Your Real Elevator Talk. -------------------------- 179
How to craft the perfect "elevator talk" --------- 183
How to increase the chance that they
will ask about your business. ---------------------- 186
Where to give your short "Elevator talk" ------- 187

Chapter 12
Keeping Track Of It All ------------------ 191
For cold calling. ------------------------------------ 191
For Referrals from Clients ------------------------ 192
Want To Know More? ------------------------------ 193

Ending 1
Recommended Reading ------------------ 197

Ending 2
About The Author ------------------------ 201

www.ClaudeWhitacre.com

Who this book is for.

I'm making a few assumptions here.
You are a salesperson whose income is determined by their sales.
You do in person sales
You are going to be doing the prospecting yourself. Although most of these methods will work with an assistant doing the prospecting, these very profitable methods will give a much better result if you do your own prospecting.
You want to generate appointments with prospects that are highly likely to buy from you.

You want to close them in one call.

Sales Prospecting By Claude Whitacre

If you sell in a prospects office/store/company, this book is for you. If you work by appointment, and sell in front of the prospect, this book is for you. If you go out looking for qualified prospects..that you can get in front of...so that they can buy from you....you have just hit the Motherload.

Who it is not for;
There are thousands of way to prospect for new customers. So I had to pick the ones that have been consistently profitable for me personally. That's going to leave some salespeople out.
If you sell industrial supplies to large companies, who buy by committee, this book isn't for you. If you make several calls to submit a proposal, and talk to the company "Buyer", this book isn't for you.

If you sell by phone, much of what you read here will be useful, but not all of it. If you sell to individuals in their home, much of this will be useful, but the cold calling section will not apply to you.

Anyone that sells to an business individual, (business owner or professional) will find just about everything will help them.

I have to get this off my chest.
When you are reading about some of these methods and approaches, the idea may occur to you, that it may sound like these ideas could be used to defraud someone.

An In-law once asked if my sales approach could be used to take advantage of someone. I said, "Not twice. Once you cheat someone, they won't buy again".

I am friends with several millionaire salespeople. Not one of them would ever do anything to jeopardize the relationship they have with their clients. Lying to make a sale, is repugnant to them. You simply can't build a lasting, solid career in sales, by misrepresenting. I've never seen it. There, I feel better now.

You still need to sell.
Although you'll be learning methods to set up appointments with prospects that are highly likely to buy, you still have to know how to sell once you are there in front of them.

This book takes you to the point where you are actually meeting the prospect. Everything after that (and a little before that) is covered nicely in **One Call Closing**.

Sales Prospecting By Claude Whitacre

"Every 'No' does not bring you closer to a 'Yes'. It just brings you closer to the next 'No'....because what you are saying, over and over again, is getting a 'No'. "

-Claude

Introduction

In my book One Call Closing, I show you how to qualify the prospect when you are in front of them, present your offer, and close. Of course, there is far more to it than that. But....

The vast majority of your sales success, is due to *who* you talk to. Not how well you close, how you dress, how dynamic you are, or how lucky you are. There is a secret all high level salespeople know, that maybe you don't. I'm going to give you the secret now.

Sales Prospecting By Claude Whitacre

Here's the secret.
Put yourself in front of prospects that have proven, in one way or another, that they are highly likely to buy from you. How to discover these prospects, and then get to see them face to face, is the entire purpose of this book. After several years of selling, it finally occurred to me that I could dramatically increase my earnings per hour, by simply increasing the odds that the person I was talking to....would buy from me, and buy that day.

You see, the first several years of selling consumers...I worked on closing sales, demonstrating my product better, and getting better at cold calling. But I didn't start making any real money, until I starting making sure I was talking to someone who was highly likely to buy from me.

This would be a better story if I just woke up one morning and made a single amazing discovery, and decided to share it with you. But reality is different. A few prospecting ideas came to me as part of working for a company. But most of these methods came slowly, and only after much testing. Everything you'll learn in this book, came to me over the course of a few decades. You are saving an enormous amount of time reading this book.

Why listen to Claude

I'm a salesman. Sure, I own a retail store, an online marketing company, and I'm a speaker/author. But at my soul, I'm a salesman. And I've been doing it nonstop for just about 40 years now. But, there are lots of experienced salespeople out there. Why listen to me?

Because I did something *very* few salespeople do. My first 25 years, I analyzed every sales presentation I made, whether they bought or not. I tried every single way you can prospect, present a product, or close. Some worked incredibly well, most ideas were flops. And I kept records of my results. My sales skills evolved. Yes, I read lots of sales books. My private library has over 1,000 printed sales books, spanning the last century. I read a new sales/marketing book every few days. But I also put the best ideas into practice. I use my businesses as labs to test new ideas. Not all new ideas are successful.

Recently, a reader asked me, "If you have been selling over 40 years, why isn't the book thicker?"

I smiled and said, "Because, all the prospecting methods that don't work well? I left them out."

Ready?

Sales Prospecting By Claude Whitacre

You are about to embark on the discovery of techniques you almost certainly have never heard before. Much that you read will contradict what you may have been taught. Much that you read will be counter-intuitive. Some of it, you may not even *like*.

But your comfort isn't my priority. Your success is.

You are going to hear the most profitable methods, to put you in front of people that are most likely to buy from you. Every figure is accurate. Every story is true. Every example is real. Every script is exactly what I use myself, today, when I sell.

Buckle up, it may get a little bumpy.

The Old Way To Sell, And Why Selling Is Frustrating And Hard.

Companies have a strong tendency to teach their salespeople to cold call. And, the reps cold call enough and eventually get a presentation. They are taught to present, answer objections, and close, close, close. After the prospect doesn't buy, they are taught to keep calling back until the prospect buys, or dies. Concentrating on finding and developing prospects that are already highly likely to buy...is very rare.

Sales Prospecting By Claude Whitacre

Are you told, by your company, to cold call? Calling strangers that are nearly guaranteed to hang up on you?

Why are you taught to cold call?
Because cold calling is easy to teach.
They don't have to do it.
Cold calling costs the company nothing.
They don't have to do it.
The company reaches new customers they never would by any other means, and.....
They don't have to do it.

We are taught to cold call, and then to present our product/service to just about anyone who will listen. This pretty well guarantees that we will be told, "No", in our presentations far more than we are told, "Yes". Not a fun way to sell. And it wears us down.

So we have endless motivational meetings. Regular sales meetings that are mostly pep rallies. Pep talks like, "We sell the best!" and, "Go get 'em Tiger!". Why? Because we are trying to lessen the agony of constant rejection. And most sales people have resigned themselves to the "fact" that selling is just an endless series of rejections and disappointments.

Wouldn't it be great if you were taught how to find and call prospects that are already proven to buy what you sell? Again, you'll get that here.

Stop Begging For Appointments.

In this book you'll discover how to only see prospects that are highly likely to buy from you on your first call. It's the difference between panning for gold, and just digging into a vein of pure gold. It's all in where you look.

Are you told to get referrals? Are you told, "You need to ask for referrals", but never hear exactly how to get high quality referrals *that actually want to talk to you*? Are you taught how to make sure your client *wants* to give you referrals? Are you taught how to have referrals expect your call, and look forward to hearing from you? Are you taught how to make sure your client looks on giving you referrals *as a favor they are doing for their friends*? Did you know that you can position "giving you referrals" as something the client will do, *to make themselves look good to their friends*? Yep. You'll learn all that here.

For most, prospecting is like roaming the countryside, looking for a few nuggets of gold. Do you know what would make that search far more profitable...and take less time? A *map*.

In your hands, you have the *map*.

"The sales doesn't begin when the customer says "No". What the heck are you saying that makes them say "No"? Stop saying it"

-Claude

Call reluctance

Let's be frank. Being told "No" over and over again just isn't fun. To many the definition of *sales prospecting* is, "Being rejected a hundred times to get one person to agree to see you".

But, what if you knew that the chance of someone agreeing to see you, when you called, was 80% to 90%? What if you knew that the person was waiting for your call, and looking forward to hearing from you? Would that make a difference? I think it would. What if, nearly everyone you met, that was a prospect...would not say, "No" to you?

Sales Prospecting By Claude Whitacre

Some would say, "Yes", but almost nobody would say, "No". You would simply not get rejected. Would that make prospecting easier?

Every method I use and teach, except one...is like that. They either say "Yes" to an appointment, or ask you a question about what you sell. That's painless prospecting. And, I think you'll enjoy it.

There is only one exception, and that is cold calling. But I'm going to show you a pretty painless way to do that too, if you choose to cold call. And, if you use the other methods shown here you really won't have to cold call.

Terrible Prospecting Ideas That Are Still Taught

You just aren't making enough calls
Managers like saying this, because it doesn't take any thought to say, "Do more". There really is a possibility that you simply aren't making enough calls. If you call three people a day..that's probably not enough. You may just need to make *better* calls. You need to make calls to people more likely to buy. Those are the calls you make first. We'll be discussing who these, "Most likely to buy", people are a little later.

Sales Prospecting By Claude Whitacre

3 foot rule.

Literally, salespeople are told to talk to everyone within three feet of them about their product or service. Really? Would you like to be on the receiving end of one of these, "Three feet", pitches?

The closest I get to this is answering questions about what I do for a living, and then leave an opening if it applies to them and they want to know more. I can't get rejected, because nobody thinks of it as a pitch. There is nothing for them to say "No" to. And I'm on my merry way. We'll be talking about the best way to do this in the section on "Elevator Talks".

Everyone is a prospect

That's a terrible thing to tell a salesperson. By thinking that everyone is a prospect, *everyone* is given equal weight. Most people are very *very* unlikely to be interested in your offer at all, and a very few are interested right now. You need to separate those two groups and concentrate on the, "Very likely to buy", prospects. We'll be talking about how to do this.

It's a numbers game

In a way, it is. If you do twice the work, you'll get twice the results. But that's not what this little bit of "wisdom" means. The thought here, is that you just plow ahead and eventually someone buys.

Personally, I don't want to present my product until I know that the prospect is almost certain to buy. I either want to find the "ready buyers", or create the situation where the prospect is pre-disposed to buying from me.

Every "No" gets you closer to a "Yes".
No. Every "No" gets you closer to another "No", because you are saying the wrong things. You are saying things that prospects say "No" to. If what you are saying generates a "No" answer, saying that exact same thing over and over again won't get you closer to a "Yes".

The only time this is true is if you are cold calling, to unqualified names, and you are running through them as fast as you can to get the "Buyers ready to buy". But do you want to be told "No" a hundred times in a row? I don't.

Sales Prospecting By Claude Whitacre

"If at first you don't succeed, try again. But don't keep trying the same thing, because you know that doesn't work"

-Claude

The One Call Closer's Prospecting System

Only present to the "Low Hanging Fruit"
There are several types of low hanging fruit when you are selling. Each will get its own chapter and you'll be able to profit from them all. Each of these sources of prospects will be different. They won't overlap.

There are prospects that are trying to find what you sell, right now. This is what we normally think of as an easy sale.

Sales Prospecting By Claude Whitacre

I tell my audiences, "Right now, in your city, there are between 10 and 100 people looking for what you sell. You need to make sure they find you". We'll be talking about cold calling a little later. It has its advantages, and it's disadvantages. And, again, you may choose to do it, or not. Every other method we talk about is only talking to interested prospects.

These are other situations that make prospects highly likely to buy.

- They bought from you before.
- They bought your product before, from someone else
- They have proven that they buy, the same way that you sell...through the same means or media.
- They will see you because their friend/associate/relative, your client, recommends you...and has bought from you....and your client has introduced you to them.
- They are contacting you because they want to buy.

This is marketing.

In conversations, they discover that you have something they want, and they ask you about it. This isn't pitching. They are asking you about what you sell.

Sources Of Customers, Best To Worst

1st Your existing customers

2nd Referrals from your happy customers

3rd Your company's existing customers

4th Your competitor's existing customers. Follow the salesman. (You're going to love this!)

5th That great customer with an immediate need. Direct mail...cold calling

6th People who buy from your method of selling… in-home, mail, referral.

7th Pretty much the other 94% of the world.

Finding high probability prospects. The turning point in my selling.
For the first several years I was in sales I knocked on doors of homeowners. At first, selling life insurance, in the late 1970's...and then selling high end vacuum cleaners for the next 25 years or so.

Sales Prospecting By Claude Whitacre

In the beginning, it never dawned on me to do anything differently. So I did presentations to anyone who would listen, and wasted a whole lot of time. I would present to people who didn't have jobs, didn't own a car, or didn't have a phone. Anyone. My sheer volume of work was enough to pay my bills, but I was treading water.

It finally dawned on me that some people were easier to sell than others. For example, if it was a married couple the chance for a sale was about 3% if the husband or wife was alone. The chance of a sale was about 40% if they were together. So, eventually, I decided to simply not present my product if both spouses weren't there. My sales increased.

Years later, While I was training a new salesperson and as we were driving to an appointment, he said something that got me thinking. He said, "What if we knew which people were going to buy, and which were not? And we could just check off the 'sure sales' on a map. Wouldn't that be great?"

I said that it sure would. But then I thought, "I've got thousands of customers. I could check off all the people that already bought from me. *I wonder what they have in common?*"

So I made it a real study, and I went over all my sales records of who bought, and who didn't...looking for common threads. I found groups of people that were far more likely to buy from me. For example, when I was selling in people's homes, if they had *already bought* from someone who did an in home presentation, the odds were much higher that they would also buy from me. If they were referred from one of my customers, they were far more likely to buy, than if they were the result of a cold call. And I found that different types of referrals gave me different results. One type of referral was almost guaranteed to buy, and another had almost no advantage over a cold call. We'll be talking about specifics later. But these differences in prospects are huge and trackable.

There were also important differences in who bought in one call. Some types of prospects required repeated calls to make a sale. And repeated calls took time. I found that certain types of prospects could be sold in one call. Eventually, I just stopped making call backs, and only saw the people who were highly likely to buy on the first call

When I was relatively new in vacuum cleaner sales, I had a friend that also sold vacuums. Occasionally, we would work together. I would do a presentation, then she would do one.

Sales Prospecting By Claude Whitacre

I didn't see her again for about ten years, and I eventually saw her at a mall. She wanted to work with me for a day again, "Just to work out some bugs". So, after the first day, she said that something was different, and she wanted to see more. She went with me on calls for a week.

At the end of that week, she told me, "Claude, do you know what's different about the way you sold ten years ago and now? Ten years ago, you would do ten presentation a week, sell two, and be happy with the two. Now, you do six presentations in a week, sell five, and agonize over why you missed the last one." And she was right. Something had changed. Sure, I was better at selling. But I was only seeing people that fell into groups that I knew would very likely buy from me.

And you know the biggest difference? If you are only selling 15-20% of your presentations, selling is work...rejection feels constant...and it just isn't all that fun.

If 80-90% of the people you see are buying, and buying on that first call? Selling is a joy. Rejection is just something others talk about. And you are getting very well paid for your time.

Creating A Web Of Buyers Out Of Highly Probable Prospects

Even if you use cold calling to get the customer, you'll want to start getting referrals from those buyers right away. And, you want that client to introduce you to their peers.

You don't want to cold call those peers. You want to be presenting your product only to people that have a high probability of buying. You want nearly everyone you present to, to buy. Why? Because anyone who talks to someone you have presented to, finds a buyer. And to that person, everyone you talk to... buys. Let's say you are presenting your product to a group of referrals in the same business, and you get a referral, that is in a different business, but he knows several people in the original niche. They still talk about you as though you are, "The guy everyone buys from". So your "circle of referrals" expands, even when you get a client from other means, like networking or cold calling.

Every time you see a prospect, it creates *A Story*. And, that story of your meeting with them gets circulated. The story can either end with anything from, "His price was way out of line, and I didn't like him much", to, "I learned a lot about how my business can use his service to increase profits, and like everyone I know, I bought his service. You should talk to him".

Sales Prospecting By Claude Whitacre

Believe me, you will be *the topic of conversation* after you talk to the prospect. You want that conversation to make the next presentation far easier, not harder. And that's why you only want to present to people highly likely to buy. It creates a great "Web of influence". Literally, everyone will be telling everyone else that buying from you is the right thing to do.

Why I recommend You Do Your Own Prospecting

- You'll know what you're getting into.
- You'll know what was actually said, to set the appointment
- A relationship will already have been started.
- It shortens the "getting to trust you" curve.
- Questions they ask while prospecting can save you a wasted appointment, or uncover an opportunity for additional sales.

Think of Prospecting as your "First Date". Would you send a friend on your first date, in your place....to save you time in getting to know the person? No. A lot can be accomplished when on a prospecting call. But it needs to be you.

Most of the methods taught here are working with very limited numbers of prospects. Each prospect is worth far more than just a name on a list. They need to be treated like the huge asset they are. For example, a short list of 5 referrals from a customer, may be worth thousands of leads from a compiled list of businesses or consumers. I learned the hard way to not give these names to a telemarketer to call for me. When you learn these methods the reasons why you will want to do this yourself will become clearer.

Is prospecting a separate sales step from presenting and closing?

Prospecting (in this book), means contacting the prospect personally to arrange an appointment. Your prospecting is the first impression the prospect has of you. Usually, just the prospecting step alone can give you a better than 50% chance of selling.

Prospecting isn't a separate step from selling. Prospecting is the first *half* of selling. So why would you trust anyone else to do that?

Scripting Or Going By Ear?

"Memorizing a short script just isn't me".
"I like to wing it. I can think pretty fast on my feet".
"I can't be loose and agile when prospecting, if I'm reading a script".

Sales Prospecting By Claude Whitacre

I hear that all the time. I understand. I used to say the same things.

Never read a script. It's almost impossible to be reading a script into a phone, and not sound like you are reading a script. Actors aren't reading a script when they are in a scene. They just remember what's in the script, and say it with emotion.

Have you ever watched a great mystery at the movies? The movies have a script. Sure, once in awhile, the actors ad lib something brilliant, but scripts that are proven, are a huge asset.

When I was in my mid 20's, I was an avid student of Kung Fu. On one of the first days, my instructor asked me to throw a punch. I did, and was pretty impressed with myself. Then he laid his palm on my shoulder, and with no apparent effort...dropped me to my knees. I asked him how he did it. I'm paraphrasing now, but here is what I remember;

"Everything you are doing right now is wrong. The way you stand, how you move, how you breath, how much effort you put into it. It's all wrong. You are fighting *yourself*. Think of how many joints you have in your body. Every joint can move in multiple directions. And every movement, either adds to the force of the strike, or takes away from it. You just need to learn the right way to move."

I asked how long that will take. He said, "Ten years, three hours a day". I took him at his word, and started serious training.

What has this got to do with selling and prospecting? Everything. There are hundreds of ways you can cold call. There are hundreds of ways you can ask for referrals. Everything you say, everything you do, either increases the chances that your prospecting will work, or increases the chance that it won't work. You want to learn the best ways *first*.

Every script I use and teach has been honed and polished by personal use, until it generates great results. Once you use the methods hundreds of times you'll start to understand the principles involved. After you understand the principles you can change what you are doing without changing the effectiveness.

The great thing is that prospecting is far simpler to learn than Kung Fu, and without the bruises.

My very best advice is to learn the language in this book. Use it until it feels comfortable. After you see results, change something. If you see better results, keep the change. If you see less results, go back to the way you were doing it.

Sales Prospecting By Claude Whitacre

I have a name for the technique of winging it. I call it "The Beginner Technique".

Maybe the most important process that will guarantee success

You need to practice. You absolutely cannot sound like you are reading a script. In fact, I'm not reading a script. My prospecting calls are so internalized that I don't need to read from a script.

But you need to practice. Have a fellow salesperson work with you. First, you be the prospect, then switch roles. Every time I learn a new technique or short script my poor wife has to listen to it over and over again. I'll use slightly different words, and she'll tell me which sounds better.

For every greeting you give a prospect, every answer you give a prospect, every approach, there is maybe one or two "best ways". I mean just one or two efficient best answers to move the appointment (or the sale) forward. Why would you ever want to play it by ear, and say, "The seventh best thing you could say"?

I have frequent conversation with a master phone salesperson. We trade ideas, and learn from each other. Once I asked if everything he said was memorized. He said, "Everything everyone says is memorized. You have to remember the word, and what it means.

Then you say the words in a certain order to get a certain response. Everything I say, over the phone, has been memorized at one point or another. Now, it just flows like a conversation. But it's a conversation that usually leads to money".

If someone asks you about what you sell..there are probably a few things that you can say that will help move a sale forward, a thousand things you can say that will hurt the sale, and one best thing to say. Why chance it? If you already knew the winning lottery numbers for tomorrow, would you just ad lib a series of numbers when playing?

No. You would use what works.

"But Claude, I've said some pretty brilliant things when winging it."

So have I. So have most of us. And occasionally, you'll say something off the cuff, that works amazingly well. And what I would do, is write it down, try to figure out why it worked, and then memorize it. Why? Because we are almost never at our sharpest. Brilliant dialog doesn't come out of our mouths 24 hours a day. These are rare "AHA" moments that need to be captured, memorized and used again.

Sales Prospecting By Claude Whitacre

That's how my prospecting dialog was built. It took years. You will get it all in its finished form, in this book.

You also need to record you calls. When you are on the phone, every little tic and snort will come out. You have to discover these, and hear solid evidence that you are saying...what you want to say. A phenomenon occurs where we think we are saying one thing, and we are saying another. In a normal conversation, we may catch it. But in talking to a prospect, we are concentrating on other things...so we sound differently than we think we do. A recording will show us how we really sound. For example, for years, I would say, "Let me ask you this..." before I asked every question. I had no idea, until I heard myself on a recording of my presentation. I also would say "OK?" after every sentence. What a monumental waste of time. And it was distracting to the prospect. I know it hurt sales. The minute I heard myself doing these things, I stopped.

Believe me, just because you're saying to yourself, "Not me, I'm not doing that", doesn't mean you sound like you think. We have a way of filtering out these little verbal mistakes.

Practice your calls. Record your actual calls. Just a few recorded calls is enough.

Your warm market.

Your warm market is people you know outside of selling. These are your friends and relatives.

Whether you contact them or not is up to you. Personally, I have sold many relatives on my side of the family, and none on my wife's side. I used a very low key approach with my own relatives. I just made it very easy to say, "No". Most said, "Sure, come on over", and all but one bought. A small part of me felt funny, because I knew that at least part of the reason they bought was because they liked me. But I also know that eventually they would all have to buy what I sold, and better from me than from a stranger. I didn't get referrals from them, because I gave them all a hefty discount, and I didn't want to end up having to give that discount to everyone they knew.

Here is an approach I use with friends and relatives;

"Bill, I've been reluctant to bring this up because we're related, and, I don't want to do anything to damage how we think of each other. But, after giving it considerable thought, I think you may be able to benefit from what I offer. Would you be open to an appointment to talk about it further? If, for any reason, you're not completely comfortable with that idea, just let me know now, and I won't have to think about it anymore."

Sales Prospecting By Claude Whitacre

There is no hesitation between the words "further" and "If". It's not really a question. I want to give them the opportunity to bow out gracefully. if they want.

If they already know what I do, and they are familiar with my service, I shorten it to;

"Bill, I've been avoiding this for awhile, but it's becoming glaringly obvious to me that my service would help you. Now, we are friends. If you want to discuss it further, let me know now. If you don't, let me know now. In any event, I can stop stewing over it".

And you know what? They usually laugh a little, and say, "I was wondering when you'd get around to it. Sure, come on over".

If they aren't interested, they will say, "That's nice that you are thinking of me. Please pass the butter". See? Nobody got mad. Nobody was nervous. They just let me know, very nicely, that they weren't a prospect. And for them, that's the end of me bringing it up.

People you buy from.

I'll be frank. I don't have any hesitation to talk to people I buy from. If they are a supplier, and I think my service (or product) applies to them, I'm much more matter of fact.

"I love the products we have been buying from you for years now. I have a service that will help you sell more of those products to guys like me. I want to discuss it with you. When is a good time this week to talk about it?". Almost every supplier we have is also a client. Almost every first advertising offer we buy, is an exchange of services. Of course, we can only do that once with each supplier, unless you have multiple offers.

When we meet I let them know that, "not buying from me", will not jeopardize our relationship.

But I wouldn't have thought of them if I didn't think it applied to their business. So, sometimes they buy, and sometimes they don't. But if they don't buy? I'm more open to a new supplier. If they do buy? That pretty much locks them in from competition.

Sales Prospecting By Claude Whitacre

Selling VS Sorting

I'm talking about prospecting. There are two approaches; Sorting and Selling.

Sorting means you are going through a list as fast as you can to find one person who is already interested in buying your product, or at least is interested in hearing more. With these prospects it's a matter of digging for gold as fast as you can..until you find gold. There is nothing wrong with this approach. We'll be talking about cold calling a little later.

Selling means that the prospect is already very likely to buy if they see your presentation. So you want them to see you. This is more often the case with referrals of buyers, and people who have proven themselves to be highly likely to buy from you, for one of several reasons. Except for cold calling, every method we discuss will be in this area. Their need for the service you sell isn't any greater than the need of people you cold call. But they are far more likely to buy from you because of factors other than "Need".

www.ClaudeWhitacre.com

Sales Prospecting By Claude Whitacre

"Right now, in your town, there are between 10 and 100 people looking to buy what you sell. You just need to find them"

-Claude

Cold Calling

My day getting cold calls
Every day at my business, I get several calls that are not from prospects or customers. I get a few recorded calls a day, and I always hang up as soon as I hear the first few words.

I get three or four calls starting with, "May I speak to the person in charge of...?" or, "May I speak to the owner please?" Sometimes, I just hang up, and sometimes I listen for a few seconds...and then I hang up.

Sales Prospecting By Claude Whitacre

But once every year or so, I get a cold call, from a live person, that sounds like a real business person. And, every so often, I buy. I'm going to share with you the cold calling process that I use. This approach would at least get me to listen for 10 seconds. In the cold calling world ten seconds is a long time. And, if I listen for ten seconds, and I hear something that interests me...there is a good chance that I'll buy. And so it is with millions of business owners.

First, Cold Calling And Canvassing? They *Work*.

For years, I was thinking of buying a million dollars in life insurance. I had just married my current wife, and we were talking about life insurance. I told her, "Honey, the first agent that calls will get my business". But, even though our marriage was in the local newspaper...no calls. Soon afterwards we opened a retail store. I said, "The opening is in the newspaper. The first insurance agent that calls will get our business". No calls! Over 100 insurance agents in our town and no calls!

We bought a new home, an expensive one, on one of the nicest streets in town. No calls.

My ads for my store were plastered all over the newspaper, blasted from radio stations, and arrived in the home of every life insurance salesman in town. No calls.

This went on for *years*. Eventually, I decided to buy my policy online. I was sitting at my office desk at my store filling out the form to buy a million dollar life insurance policy.

At that exact moment a man walked into our store, and I walked out onto the sales floor to see what I could do for him. He said, "I'm with New York Life. Who do you have your life insurance with?"

And I pointed at him and said, "You!". I think I scared him a little.

The yearly premium was about $5,000. I know it was probably the largest commission this man had ever made, and certainly the fastest.

Why am I telling you this?

Because in your town, today, there are between 10 and 100 people who want to buy what you sell. You just need to sort through and find them. The sales will be almost effortless.

The process of sifting through all those people in the fastest way possible, is called Cold Calling.

Sales Prospecting By Claude Whitacre

Advantages of cold calling;
You get new blood. New customers that will give you referrals and buy again. You'll get customers you wouldn't get in any other way.

The approach is transactional. Meaning they are thinking of your product, not you. This is not a relationship sale. It's a matter of being "at the right place at the right time".

It takes less skill to sell someone already looking to buy.

Disadvantages of cold calling;
It takes time to find people that were thinking of buying your product/service right now. You may have to contact 100 or more people before you find your first buyer.

You need a big list. One thousand names and phone numbers at least. 5,000 is better. That way, it won't matter if this particular person says, "No".

A lesson I learned from a terrible salesperson.
After I had been selling vacuum cleaners in people homes for a decade or so I began having salespeople approach me to learn how I did so well.

This young man stopped by my office one day and asked if I could teach him how to sell. He sold another brand of vacuum cleaner.

I asked him a few questions.

"How many have you sold so far?" He said, "Three". I asked, "What is your closing percentage?". He said "100%".

It kind of surprised me. So I asked, "How did you get 100% of your presentations to buy? Tell me about your experience"

He told me that he talked to 300 people at their doors. Three let him in to talk to them, and all three bought.

So I asked, "What did you say at the door?", and this is what he told me...

"Hi. I sell a vacuum cleaner made by Amway. It costs $899. Would you like me to show it to you?". I swear, that was what he told them. And three out of 300 said, "Sure, come on in."

I had to give this a little thought. This young man knew nothing about selling. It was like a foreign language to him, but he sold 100% of the people he presented his product to.

The problem was, I didn't sell that brand, and he wasn't willing to switch to my product, no matter how much more money he would have made. So we parted ways after one discussion.

Sales Prospecting By Claude Whitacre

But what I learned is that if you just want to make the super easy sales, you can just talk to enough people to find the really interested ones. And one in 100 sounds about right.

Call Reluctance When Cold Calling

This happens far more when doing cold calling. But, you can also have a bout of "call reluctance" when you just don't feel like calling your referrals. It's that feeling in the pit of your stomach that you'll be told, "No", and you'll take it personally.

Pretend that you are doing a survey. You are calling people and asking, "Do you like french fries?"

Could you do that, if it paid well enough? In my speeches I ask that question, and almost every hand goes up. Why is that? Because you don't care what the answer is. You don't *care* if they like french fries. You just want the answer. It isn't personal.

If I showed you a deck of cards, face down...and said, "Start flipping these cards over. Every time you get an Ace, I'll give you $100. Every time you get a different card, you owe me nothing, but you get nothing. And we can do this with as many decks of cards as you like"..what would you do? Would you accept? Of course you would. And you would flip the cards over as quickly as you could, to find an Ace. You would do it all day. Why?

Because, when you get a card that isn't an Ace, you don't take it personally.

One way to cold call is to try to build a relationship over the phone, and then try for an appointment. The reason I don't favor this approach, is that the rejection will feel personal. I only cold call with a "transactional offer". They are either immediately interested, or they are not. If they are interested it isn't because of your amazing personality, and if they are not interested it isn't because they don't like you. And it's very, *very* fast.

When cold calling, why you only want to present to the Low Hanging Fruit

Cold calling is about the offer/the service you sell. It isn't about brand building. Prospects won't talk about you if you cold call them because the call happens too fast for them to remember anything about you or your company. But they remember you and your company when you present to them. So you want to only present, from cold calls, the prospects highly likely to buy. This starts the entire chain of linked buyers.

Sales Prospecting By Claude Whitacre

I'll be showing you my method to cold call...if you choose to cold call...and it's pretty painless. You won't be taking the "No" personally, because it won't be directed at you. You may even enjoy it.

Let's get to it.

A Cold Calling "Aha" Moment

Years ago, when I was selling vacuum cleaners I was cold calling by knocking on doors. It was unpleasant work. Nobody is happy to see you when you are knocking on their door.

Anyway, it was the last day of the month, and I was in a contest. A storm was going to arrive within the hour, and canvassing in a storm is a no-no. I needed a sale. One more sale would give me a huge bonus for the month.

I kind of panicked. I started running from door to door. I wasn't looking for someone to let me demonstrate my vacuum cleaner, I was looking for a sale. So all my training went out the window. I knocked on doors and said approximately the following, "Hi, I sell vacuum cleaners. If you take a look at mine, I'll give you this cutlery set. Are you thinking about getting a new vacuum cleaner?"

That last sentence was a killer. It made most people turn me down. But I needed a sale, not a demonstration.

After about forty five minutes a man said, "Sure, if it's good enough, we could use a better vacuum cleaner".

After I brought the machine in their home, I told him and his wife that I was in a contest, and that I couldn't spend time showing the vacuum cleaner unless there was a real possibility of a sale that night. He said, "Sure, like I said, we're interested in what you have".

Of course, they bought (Thank Goodness). I won my contest. But what I gained, that was far more valuable, was the realization that there are actually people out there that want what you have right now. And, as much as you are looking for them, they are looking for you. My job was just to find them. This changed my cold calling procedure forever.

Whether I was knocking on doors (this was in the 1970-1980s), or calling on the phone, I found that it was much more profitable if I concentrated on finding the one or two people, that day, that were truly ready to buy what I sold. Rather than trying to convince prospects to let me talk to them, and then convince them to buy, it was easier to just quickly sort through the list, to find the ideal buyers.

This idea only works if you have a near unlimited supply of prospects. For example, in my area, we had 20,000 people I could call.

Sales Prospecting By Claude Whitacre

If you sell a highly specialized product that is only bought by a very small segment of the market, I wouldn't do this. Instead, I would concentrate on building a relationship with the few possible buyers you have to work with.

The big advantage of this "call quickly to find the best buyer" method is that you don't really care if any one person is interested in what you have. You are actually trying to dis-qualify the people you talk to as quickly as you can. Phoning prospects rapidly is also a key to this. If you call three people an hour, you'll spend an entire day, and maybe not even set one appointment.

If you call prospects as quickly as possible, you'll find that time flies. You'll also end up with several appointments with highly qualified and eager buyers.

The Best Cold Call I Ever Received.
I was busy at work, the phone rings, I picked it up. This was several years ago.

Him; "Claude?"
Me; "Yes, what can I do for you?"
Him; "I sell long distance for 4 cents a minute. Do you want to know more?"
Me; "Yes"

Here's why I loved that cold call;
It was fast. I know he was calling at least 100 places an hour. Most would say "No" to his question, but it wasn't personal, it was saying "No" to switching your long distance company.

And when I said "Yes", that meant that I was already agreeing to his proposition. Some propositions aren't as easy to explain, but usually one sentence will do it.

Another reason I like the call? I could get back to work. There was no need to ask, "How are you?", or try to engage me in conversation. It was a simple transactional offer. I'm guessing that he had at least one person per hour buy, and he was only talking further...to the buyers.

The Secret To Guaranteeing That Your Cold Calling Is Profitable
Phone faster..in 1 hours time you'll get a couple of solid appointments if you phone fast. Then you'll say, "Wow, this works". If you call only a few every hour, it will feel like you never get an appointment. "It doesn't work..I called for a whole hour!". Phone faster.

May I suggest a company? I use Callfire as the service to help me make very fast calls to large lists of prospects.

Sales Prospecting By Claude Whitacre

Just go to callfire.com for more information. A huge advantage of using a dialing service like Callfire, is that as soon as you hang up, the next number is automatically dialed for you. There is no way to procrastinate between calls.

If you want lists of businesses that are local, and you want the names that are listed in online directories, may I suggest using Mobile Renegade. It's a software that pulls business listings out of online listings, and builds you a list to call. It's very useful if you are selling to local business people. You can go to mobilerenegade.net. But! You may be able to find it cheaper from another source.

Cold Calling; how much do you qualify on the phone?

How long does a presentation take, including drive time? How many potential prospects do you have? Determine how much to qualify before you see them.

Calling out of a directory by street, where each appointment is only a few minutes away from another appointment? I may not qualify except that the person I'm talking to is the owner of the business. Because I'll schedule those appointments very close together...maybe one every 15 minutes. And if there is anything I don't like, I'm on my way to the next appointment.

But a 3 hour consultation on site to sell a high dollar marketing service? Nearly all qualifying is done on the phone.

When I get call-in leads. All qualifying is done on the phone. Because they contacted me, and are ready to buy. I just want to make sure they are a fit for what I do.

Supercharge your results. Add a limitation that qualifies your best customers.
Eventually, I learned that I would dramatically increase my cold calling appointments if I added a limiting factor, or a qualification at the end of my benefit statement. Let's imagine I was calling you selling long distance for 4 cents a minute. I would say, "I sell long distance for 4 cents a minute, but only if you own a small business. Would you like to know more?"

Here's why "...but only if you own a small business" helps; It makes the offer sound harder to get. It make you sound selective. It also forces the prospect to think, "Why do I need to be a small business owner?", and they may ask.

It makes it sound like I may turn them down.

Sales Prospecting By Claude Whitacre

Why don't I mind saying, "but only for small business owners"? *Because I'm calling a list of small business owners.* To them, the offer sounds exclusive, but the niche is virtually everyone I'm calling.

Let's try another one.

Here is my cold calling benefit statement. "I create quality leads and sales for business owners that already have a website. Would you like to know more?". Now, why do I say, "that already have a website"? Because every business that does any business at all, already has a website. And the excuse they used to give me was, "We already have a website".

So I just added it to my "benefit statement". And now when I say it to a prospect they are asking themselves, "I wonder why he only works with people that already have a website? I already have a website. Maybe this is specifically for me. Maybe I should talk to this guy."

This won't cause everyone to make an appointment. But it may increase your appointments from one qualified appointment, per hour of calling, to two, per hour of calling. So it's very much worth doing.

Cold calling scripts;

"Hi, I (benefit statement). (limiting condition) Would you like to know more?" Use only for a very easy to explain service. You are just looking for that guy that's thinking about buying right now.

Sample Benefit Statements with a limiting statement;

"help small business owners save 50% on their shipping costs, if they ship 25 or more packages a month".

"guarantee credit card processing for 25% less than you are paying now, but only for brick and mortar businesses".

"print business cards with your photo in full color for only a dime each. But only in packs of a thousand".

"provide skilled part time workers on 24 hour notice, to offices in Fort Worth only".

"provide life insurance at preferred rates, to non-smokers only".

So I would say, "Hi; Claude Whitacre here. Could I speak with Bob please?". "Hi Bob, I provide life insurance at preferred rates, to non-smokers only. Would you like to know more?".

Sales Prospecting By Claude Whitacre

Instead of saying, "Would you like to know more?", you can also use, "Would that be of value to you?'.

Now, I only call small business owners, and I know the owner's name before I call. That's part of the information I get when I buy lists to call. I use Infousa.com for my lists. I've heard that Infofree.com is also a good source for sales leads.

If you are calling a business. Know your contact's name.

Never say, "May I speak to the owner, please?". That's like screaming, "Hang up on me now!"

So you need to know the name of the person you want to talk to.
But... if you don't know, say, "I need your help. I want to talk to the owner, but I don't have their name with me. Could I get it please?" They will either transfer you, ask what you want, or say "No". Get off the phone and call back later with the name.

This is my approach when calling event planners to book a speaking gig.

"Hi. Claude Whitacre here. Could I speak with Bob Jones please?" and sound like my name means something. "Bob here" "Bob, this is Claude Whitacre. I understand that you're the one responsible for booking speakers for your trade show in February, is that right?"

"Yes, what can I do for you?"

"Well, I give a talk on how your Trade Association members can get seen online, and attract a line of eager buyers, at no cost to them. But only if they have a brick and mortar business. Does that sound like something that would be of value to your members?" (Yes)

"Then I have something you'll like. Do you have a minute right now, or should I call back?"

"No, I have a minute right now. Tell me about your talk."

The reason I ask, "Do you have a minute right now, or should I call back?" is that it's something a friend would ask, and I don't want them telling *me*, half way through the conversation, that they have to go. And almost always, they say, "Sure, I have a minute. Go ahead".

I always want to know the contact's name before I call. If I'm calling without the name, now I need to make two calls. It's worth the few extra pennies per name to get the owner's name.

If you sell something that doesn't apply to everyone you call, you can add a layer to make sure you are talking about something that applies to them.

Sales Prospecting By Claude Whitacre

Here's a real life example from my core business, taken from a transcript.

"Hi. Claude Whitacre here. Could I speak with Bob Jones please?"

"Bob here"

"Bob, this is Claude Whitacre. I understand that you're the one responsible for advertising for your business, is that right?"

"Yes"

"First, do you have a quick minute, or are you with a customer?"

"I have a quick minute"

"Do you ever get customers that say they found you online?"

"Sure, on occasion"

"Would you like more of them?"

"What's this about?"

"I provide quality leads and sales to business owners that already have a website. Would you like to know more?"

"How do you do that?"

"Well, I see to it that your business is more easily found online, and your competitors are less easily found online. Does that sound like something that would be of value to you?"

"Maybe. How much does it cost?"

"It costs you nothing to find out more. And I have something you'll want to see. Will you be available at your business tomorrow at 3PM?"

"How long will this take?"

"Ten minutes, unless you have questions. Will you be there at 3?

"Sure".

"Looking forward to meeting you".

Now, let's break down every line. Because if you leave anything out, you hurt your chances of an appointment. If you add much more, it also hurts your chances.

"Hi. Claude Whitacre here. Could I speak with Bob Jones please?"
You should know the name of the person you're asking for. Mailing lists and directories usually have the company officer list as part of the company listing.

Sales Prospecting By Claude Whitacre

If you don't know who to ask for, here's what works; "Hello, could you help me? I lost the name of the person in charge of ___. Who would that be, please?" And after they tell you, just say, "Thank you" and hang up. Call back in a few days, and ask for the person by name. Never call blindly and ask, "Can I speak to the owner please?". Those calls nearly always get nowhere.

Personally, I say my name like I expect them to have heard of me. Nearly always, I just get through, or get Bob's voice mail. If I get the voice mail, I just call back another time.

"Bob, this is Claude Whitacre. I was told that you're the one responsible for ___, is that right?"
I just want to verify that I'm talking to the right person. And it sounds like I already know the answer. This is the only step I ever skip, if I'm sure he's the right one to talk to.

"First, do you have a quick minute, or are you with a customer? (or client, patient)"
I get salespeople asking me why I ask this question. Because it shows that I know I could be interrupting something. And I could be. Usually, I get an answer like, "Go ahead. What can I do for you?" I'm generally calling retailers that are talking to customers all day.

If I were calling Real Estate Agents, or Life Insurance Agents, I would skip this step. And it's something a friend would ask when they are calling.

"Do you ever get customers that say they found you online?"
This is a qualifying question that asks if we are likely to be a match. It's also a way for Bob to just say "No". I want it easy for Bob to say "No". I'm only looking for low hanging fruit.

"Would you like more of them?"
I ask this question in a very lighthearted way. As though I know he's going to say "Yes".

This is the question they must answer "Yes" to, before I continue. If they answer "No", I don't ask why. I just let them go. At this stage, I'm not trying to convince anyone, I'm just looking for that easy sale.

"Well, I ____. Does that sound like something that would be of value to you?"
A question here is OK. But then I just answer the question, and then repeat this, "..be of value?" question back to them. The second time I say it, I may even add, "It's Ok if the answer is No".

Again, I'm not convincing, I'm sorting.

59

Sales Prospecting By Claude Whitacre

"Well, I see to it that your business is more easily found online, and your competitors are less easily found online. Does that sound like something that would be of value to you?"
I will give one objection an answer. He asked a reasonable question, so I gave a general answer that moves the process along. When I ask, "Does that sound like something that would be of value to you?" ..he has to say "Yes" to that, or I move to the next call. Of course, if he didn't ask me, "How do you do that?" I would skip this part, and just go to.....

"Then I have something you'll want to see. Will you be available tomorrow at about 3PM?"
And here is where you may get a stall. "Can you just mail me the information?", "I'm very busy this month", "We are happy with our current supplier"...or something along those lines.

I don't mind one stall, but if there is more than one, the conversation is now turning into "Me convincing him" and I don't want that. So I may say, "It sounds like you don't want me to show up. Is that right?". Now, he'll either give in, or (more likely) disengage.

I only cold call for local companies. Why? Because the average quality of the appointment is less than a referral. And I don't want to waste much time. So I'll drive maybe 15 minutes for a cold call appointment, but not an hour.

Now, if I were selling something that didn't require that I meet with the prospect, the entire selling sequence would be done over the phone, hopefully on that one call.

And you'll notice that my example was a little more complicated than what I'm telling you to do. If I were calling a list of life insurance agents, here is the entire conversation.

"Hi, Claude Whitacre calling for Bob Jones"

"This is Bob, what can I do for you?"

"Bob, I supply life insurance agents with qualified leads and buyers, to agents that already have a website. Would you like to know more?"

You can very easily adapt this to any offer you have.

I can make the call much faster, because I know that he's not with a client (if he was, he would let the call go to voice mail)

Sales Prospecting By Claude Whitacre

If You Want To Fill Your Day With Local Appointments.

I almost didn't want to include this technique in this book, because I reserve it for my consulting clients. I use it to fill my day with places to go. I do no qualifying on the phone, except for my one conditional statement, and to verify that the owner will be there. Then I just go rapidly from appointment to appointment. In 5 hours of cold calling last week (over two days), I used this exact approach.

I called 80 businesses in a town close to mine. I had 51 contacts with the business owners, I set 15 appointments, 7 were there to talk to me when I arrived. I did a complete presentation with three of them. Two bought. One for $5,999 and one for $3,999. The only reason I would stop this process, is because I get so busy, it can be exhausting. So I use it more sparingly now. But if you are in a sales contest. This is the Quota Buster. Here it is;

"Hello, Bob? Claude Whitacre here. I create quality leads and sales for business owners that already have a website. *I'm not calling for an appointment, but I'd like to drop off some information for you to look at, and meet you for 5 minutes. If you decide to set up an appointment down the road, that's up to you. Fair Enough?*"

The "Um..sure"

Me; "Great, will you be there between 2 and 3 PM tomorrow? I'll be dashing in and out pretty quick. I look forward to meeting you."

See? There is almost nothing to say "No" to. It's very hard to say, "No, I refuse to meet you for 5 minutes". Of course, once you are talking to them, you'll both know very quickly if you have a reason to stay. And almost never do you make an appointment for later. You just talk to them there.

The reason it works so well is that they can't say "No" to an appointment, because you just said you weren't calling for an appointment. To be fair, this techniques is just a little sneaky. But I've never had a prospect mention it or complain.

And of course, you can adapt this approach very easily, for any offer. I only use it when I have a directory where the listings are very close together geographically. I wouldn't drive for 20 minutes for this kind of lead. I'll set maybe 3 appointments in every one hour block. I breeze through these very quickly. I called all of these myself. I once hired a telemarketer, but quickly saw that they were getting a small fraction of the results. It's much easier to say "No" to "My manager wants to meet you" than to "I want to meet you".

Sales Prospecting By Claude Whitacre

Objections. Should you handle them?

A common response is to ask you to just send information. This is just a stall. This is a reflexive response that they give to *every* person calling for an appointment.

"Can you send me some information?"

"No. I want to meet you. After we talk for 5 minutes, you can decide if we should schedule an appointment later. Will you be there tomorrow at 3PM?" See? I'm not even asking them for an appointment, just a chance to meet them. There is very little to say "No" to. I picked up the idea in a sales book, I think. No idea which one.

I'm not kidding, about a third of the time, they say OK.

And, here's what I say after every objection to an appointment.

"I'm busy all this month"

"So am I, so I can't take much time. We'll know after ten minutes if this is something to talk further about. Will you be there tomorrow at 3PM?"

"I'm happy with what I have now".

Me; "Then what we have will fit you nicely. We should meet. Will you be there at 3PM tomorrow?"

Years ago, I was thinking about how kids ask their parent's to get ice cream.... "Mom, I want, Mom, I want, Mom, I want...." And then the mom just says OK. It just popped into my little brain.

See, the objections aren't real. They are a reflex. That's why having the perfect answer doesn't work. You are battling something that doesn't exist.

Imagine that you asked a girl on a date;

"I'm sorry, that night, I'm washing my hair"..

So now, you start talking about how she shampoos her hair, how long it takes to dry....Why isn't this working? Because the objection wasn't real. And when you try to answer that objection, it isn't registering with the prospect. They aren't thinking of their objection when you are answering it. They have already moved on to another thought. Usually, what other objection they can think of, to get you off the phone politely.

My saying, "We should meet. Will you be there tomorrow at 3PM?" works for one simple reason. There is nothing to say "No" to. There is no rebuttal that makes sense. All they can do is say, "Not interested, bye!" and hang up before you say, "Not interested? Then we have to meet. Will you be there tomorrow at 3PM?"

Sales Prospecting By Claude Whitacre

About one out of three calls have resulted in an appointment. That's my personal experience.

And when you are taught to cold call, in a way that gets you an appointment once out of every one hundred calls, this approach feels like a breeze.

I'll answer two stalls. I found that after the first couple of objections, it degrades into a contest, a contest I don't want to play. Once they start pulling away from you, the momentum of the call is going away from you. It's nearly impossible to get these people to become interested again.

I never call anyone back. I'm just asking for an appointment, not for a donated kidney.

If they can't decide on an appointment, I'm not interested in them. You will get some appointments with these "Call me back later" prospects, but you'll get far better results, per call, by just calling the next number on your list. Why? Because usually, it's a stall. And the next time you call, it will be a stall. And now you are chasing them. And chasing someone causes them to run away. You don't want to be positioning yourself as the pesky salesperson, that really needs to make the sale.

I would never use this to close a sale, but to get an appointment? Absolutely.

Again, I'll generally answer two questions, but if they keep asking questions, or give objections, I lose interest fast. But it's your choice.

A major question you should ask yourself is; "How much time am I willing to invest in a cold call, before I give up?" My advice is, go for the easy appointment. You are looking for people that are open to your offer, today.

And it's far easier on you if you are just asking a qualifying question, getting either a "Yes" or a "No". Spending ten minutes on the phone with someone, bantering back and forth, failing to get an appointment can be frustrating. Go for the easy appointments.

If they give you a specific objection that isn't a stall

Some objections aren't stalls. If they say, "Interesting, but I just bought a large insurance policy" or, "Well, I already have a great supplier for that", you can say, "Based on what you've just told me, I think we *should* get together. Tomorrow at 3PM?". Now, don't say that if their condition makes the appointment undesirable to you. You don't want to see everybody.

Sales Prospecting By Claude Whitacre

If he says, "Well, we are closing our doors for good at the end of the month" you don't want to say, "Based on what you've just told me, I think we *should* get together. Tomorrow at 3PM?".That would be silly.

If you get a "gatekeeper"
To be perfectly upfront, I almost never get this. I don't generally sell to large corporations, that have assistants. And in the rare case that I do, they know who I am. But I recently read this in the book **Cold Calling Techniques That Really Work** by Stephen Schiffman. I tried it twice, and it got me through both times. The gatekeeper asks, "What's this call concerning?' And I just say, "Do you want to hear the *whole* story?". Both times, they said, "I'll put you through".

If You Have To Cancel An Appointment, Or If They Postpone It
Cancelled appointments that reschedule buy at a higher percentage because they have had more exposure to you....even if it's on the phone. The more times they talk to you, or talk to others about you, before you show up? The better the chance they will buy from you. It's because they are getting used to having you in their life.

Cold walking

Whether you are talking to consumers or business owners, the approach is basically the same as on the phone. I like going business to business, because I fall into sales, on the spot. And I make it so easy to say "No" to me. My thought is that one in every ten businesses (where I talk to the owner), will be a sale. I just need to know which one that is. So, I'm really just looking for that one nice guy that is willing to listen, and qualifies as a real prospect.

The Irresistible Bribe. Prospecting that creates a feeding frenzy.

Do you want prospect falling all over each other to talk to you? When I sold vacuum cleaners by knocking on people's doors, I literally would say, "I'm just doing a quick survey, may I ask you a few questions?" Maybe half of the people would ask me inside. If it was snowing, nearly everyone asked me inside. If it was raining, less often.

As soon as I got in the home, I asked several questions that sounded like regular survey questions, but were really qualifying questions. For example;

"Is this your home?"

"What kind of work do you do?"

"Do you have pets"

Sales Prospecting By Claude Whitacre

"Do you have allergies?"

"What kind of vacuum cleaner are you using right now?"

If anything wasn't what I wanted to hear, I thanked them and left. If I decided that I wanted to give them a presentation, I would simply offer a gift, for letting me show them my vacuum cleaner. My best gift was a small portable TV that I bought from an importer for $28 or so. As soon as I offered it, nearly everyone took the offer. So I had to offer it only *after* I decided I wanted to talk to them. People would postpone supper and even skip a football game, for a free portable TV.

About half of the people I gave the TV to, bought. My cost for the gift was roughly $56 *per sale*. But I was making $1,000 a sale, so it was worth it.

The approach helped because everyone has a vacuum cleaner, and most people aren't thinking of buying one before you get there. But the presentation would get roughly 50% to buy, no matter what they were thinking before you showed up.

I've used gifts for small business owners too. It makes it easier to see them, but some industries frown on it. So you have to be in an industry that allows gift giving, and you have to be selling to an industry that allows getting gifts from suppliers.

I stopped giving gifts when I found out that you could get appointments without it. But it made cold calling a little easier.

When I'm selling online marketing services to business owners, it's far less likely that a gift will help. The prospects have to be open to local online marketing services, and that's a little less than 10% of the people that own small businesses. So I really want to know if they are interested in my service, not just interested in a gift. So, I don't use a gift.

A client of mine does commercial cleaning of bathrooms in restaurants and other businesses. He offers to clean a bathroom for free as a sample. Of course, most every restaurant has a men's and ladies' room. So the owner would see a huge difference, and pay for the other restroom, and then a contract would ensue. I signed up for the service myself.

Sales Prospecting By Claude Whitacre

"I don't want to annoy people"
Many, with the goal of "not wanting to annoy people," water down what they say and ease into a call with ridiculous questions like, "How are you?" or, "Do you have a minute?"

If you do not want to annoy people, then be brief, be concise, and find out if they are interested in as few words as possible. Do you know what annoys prospects? Beating around the bush.... Not getting to the point....Asking, "How are you" and, "How's the weather up there?".

Don't water down what you are saying, because you do not want to annoy people.

Here is a list of things that cold callers say at the beginning, that is simply a waste of time;

"How are you today?"

"Hi, are they working you hard today?"

"How's the weather up there in Ohio?"

"Do you have a minute, or are you busy?"

There is only one reason I ask, "Do you have a minute?" is if they own a retail store, and they may be with a customer. And I only ask if the conversation is going to last several minutes.

In most cold calls asking, "Do you have a minute, or are you in the middle of something?" actually takes maybe 20 seconds. If your total call time is going to be one minute, now it's 45% longer than it needs to be. You're wasting time on every call. Stop it!

Time waster in the middle of a cold call;
"We want to see what we can do for you."

"We want to make an appointment, to tell you about the services we offer, and to see if there is anything we can do to help you."

"We offer several services that you may not be aware of...."

"We offer multiple products that many find useful"

Only talk about one thing at a time. General statements like, "We offer a multitude of options in...", isn't going to help you get an appointment. Be concise. "We want to tell you about the services we offer", doesn't fulfil a need on the prospect's end. It doesn't create desire to meet with you. Leave out the general talk that describes nothing.

Time wasters at the end of cold calls;
"It was great talking to you. You have a nice day now. OK?"

"Have a safe drive home and a great weekend."

Sales Prospecting By Claude Whitacre

"Are you sure you're not interested?"

I had a cold calling appointment setter once ask everyone that didn't want to set an appointment, "Are you sure you aren't interested?". I listened to her, and asked, "How many calls have you made since you started here?" She said, "Oh, it's hard to say...maybe a thousand".

I asked her how many she said, "Are you sure you aren't interested?" to have the prospect turn around and say, "You know, now that I think about it...I *am* interested"? The answer, of course, was none.

Twenty percent of her time on the phone with non-buyers was spent asking this nice homey question. Then, of course, she would say, "You all have a nice day now". Tick, tick, tick....

Be friendly. Speak in a friendly tone. These people were doing something when you called and they want to get back to it as soon as possible. So shave off all the unnecessary verbiage.

Do you say things like, "Let me ask you this," or say, "Right?" at the end of every sentence? These little verbal trips are time wasters, and are annoying to the listener.

Think of sales prospecting as prospecting for gold. One of the best things you can do is separate the gold from the mud as fast as you can.

When setting sales appointments, clear and concise delivery is you goal. Keep it as short as possible.

Here is the main reason you want the call to be brief. The more you talk, the more opportunity the prospect has to think of a reason that he/she doesn't need what you sell, or that now isn't the right time.

Sending Direct Mail Before You Call
Don't do it. Almost never have they read your letter. If they have read it, they won't be thinking about it when you call. And, here is what you'll say, "Hi, it's Bob Franks from ACME Tools. I sent you a letter. Did you get a chance to read it?" Everything from there on is a trap. They will nearly always say, "Nope. Didn't read it". Now you'll have to tell him about what was in this letter he didn't read. Or, he will say, "Nope, didn't read it. Send it again". What a waste of time.

If it makes you feel better about this, I mailed sales letters for several months and then I would call them to make an appointment. Once, I forgot to mail the letters and called them anyway. The percentage of appointments I made was identical. Not any change at all.

I didn't have to pay to mail a sales letter. I didn't have to time my call to a letter they never read. My calls were faster, and far less clunky.

Sales Prospecting By Claude Whitacre

There are two other approaches for cold calling on the phone. I don't use them but I'll address them here, because you'll eventually think of them yourself.

Call, send, call.
There are salespeople that do this. They call to ask if they can send over a brochure, email a video, or some other information. The prospect gets the information, and the salesperson calls back to answer any questions.

I did this myself for a short time. I stopped when I realized that I was selling the same number of people, if I simply called once to make the appointment. The only part I use is that, after I make the appointment, I'll send over some information...before I see them. This way, I'll be slightly more familiar to them, and it will help sculpt the questions they ask. It also establishes me as more of an expert, assuming they look at what I send them.

3 call technique

In the "selling stocks over the phone" industry, there is a way they sell that should be mentioned.

They make three phone calls, and they go like this;

First call; "Hello, Mr. Whitacre, I'm Bob with Sellstocks Inc. I don't have any trading advice today, but is it OK if I call you when we have a good stock to recommend?"

Second call a few days later; "Hello, Bob here. I just wanted to touch base with you. I don't have a stock to recommend today, but I'm keeping you in mind".

Third call "Claude? Bob here. I found it, the stock that I think you should look at. Let me tell you about it..." I'm paraphrasing here.

The language may be a little different. But the three steps are the same. The purpose of the first two calls is to start a "relationship" and build a little trust.

I've never used this method, and I don't know the results of using this three step method. But I wanted to make you aware of it.

Why you need other methods of prospecting besides cold calling.

How many know they need what you sell, and are ready to buy right now? 1 in 100? One in 200? How many will see you if you have a great cold calling script, and know how to handle objections?

Maybe one in three or one in six. How many qualified prospects would want your product, if they knew all about it, and trusted your recommendation? Five in ten? Eight in ten? That's why we need other ways of prospecting in addition to cold calling.

www.ClaudeWhitacre.com

"With referrals, it isn't about helping you. It isn't even about helping the referral. Everything centers on the promise you made to the client, to give the referral your time"

-Claude

Referrals

Benefits of referrals;
There are many benefits to properly getting and seeing referrals from your current clients.

You start at a higher point of trust. The acceptance of your recommendation is nearly assured with a properly introduced referral.

Your price is less of an issue because you are no longer selling just a commodity. The relationship has value now, the trust has value.

Sales Prospecting By Claude Whitacre

On the other hand, it's your obligation not to take advantage of this relationship by charging more than you normally would.

The sale moves faster. They buy quicker because the part of selling where you are establishing trust and common ground is mostly done when you begin the presentation. Buying from you (from the prospect's point of view) is already something that feels like a natural result of meeting you.

You'll close a far higher percentage of sales with referrals, than through cold leads. My closing ratio with introduced referrals is typically 90% or better. The prospect is now looking for reasons to buy from you. Partly to keep rapport with the person who introduced you, as long as they are a client also..

Depending on what you sell your average sale size is larger with referrals. They are less likely to give you a small "trial order", and just buy what you recommend.

Clients you obtained through a referral are far more likely to give you better quality referrals as part of the interview. To them, it's just part of the process. And they are very likely to give you more referrals over time. There are treasured relationships. Don't abuse them. Keep the referral source in the loop.

Because the introduced referrals are far more likely to see you , and buy from you....the "stress" of rejection is minimized. And some of these referrals will become real friends.

Referred sales take less time, are easier to deal with, and stay as customers longer. Referrals create a "web of consensus". Prospecting by getting referrals in niches or in families, creates "Buzz". The members are rather expected to talk to you, and are expected to buy. Imagine if 5 co-workers each told you, "You really need to talk to this guy", and then they went on to tell you how this person made them a great offer, and took care of them. You would almost certainly see this person, out of curiosity and to keep in "The club". How would you like to be the salesperson on your way to see the 8th person in this niche, and the other seven have bought and talked about you? That's the power of referrals.

When I saw the difference between cold calling and selling by referrals.
In 1981, there was a recession in the United States. At the time, I had a large organization selling vacuum cleaners. I got a call one day from our source of financing. No more financing, until the economy got better. So I had to sell something that didn't require financing to make the sale. I became an Insurance agent for a popular insurance company.

Sales Prospecting By Claude Whitacre

My second month, I was the top agent in the office. And I stayed at, or near, the top every month for a year. I didn't talk to the other agents, except at the weekly sales meetings. Our manager would have us hand in our numbers for the week, and we would get "motivated".

To be fair, I was just getting referrals from past customers, and selling insurance to them, and selling to employees at local companies. It was very easy for me. And I was used to making a great living selling. I had already been selling for over 8 years, and doing well. I didn't really struggle.

So, at the meeting, we would all give the number of people we called, the number of presentations we made, and the number of applications handed in.

Whitacre is usually the last name alphabetically in any group, so I would go last.

First guy;
"245 calls, 26 presentations, zero sales."

Second guy,
"175 calls, 14 presentations, one sale"

Third guy,
"173 calls, 15 presentations, and one sale"

It would go on like that with maybe 12 agents. The I'd say "7 calls, 6 presentations, 5 sales".

And it would go on like that week after week. One week I wrote everyone in a small company. So my figures were "5 calls, 17 presentations, 17 sales".

Eventually, it got to me. So I stood up and said, "Doesn't anyone want to know how I make all these sales, with so few calls? All of you guys are either terrible at selling, or you are outright liars.. It's impossible to talk to ten people and not sell one. Doesn't anyone want to know how I make as many sales a week, as the rest of you combined?"

I wasn't popular. The manager actually told me that I no longer needed to show up for the sales meetings. I'm assuming that you want to know how I did it. I only worked by referral. And the client had to introduce me to their referrals. I wasn't just asking for referrals. I was asking the client about the referral. I was asking the client to contact the referral for me, to make sure they were willing to talk to me...and I only talked to people with good jobs and the ability to buy from me.

Anyway, at the end of a year selling life insurance I got a call from my financing source telling me that they were back to financing my vacuum cleaners. So I left the agency, and became a factory direct, vacuum cleaner distributor again.

85

Levels of trust and how it related to referrals.

I dislike seeing part of a book, used in a different book, by the same author. But here we are. The Layers Of Trust list, was also in my book **One Call Closing**.

But now we will see how it applies to referrals and prospecting.

Every level up is at least twice as hard to achieve as the level directly below it. Most salespeople are seen by their customers at the bottom three levels. From level four and higher, you're making easier sales, for more money, to people who trust you. But you have to earn that trust. This has nothing to do with misrepresenting.

Seven levels of Trust; Best to worst...

1) Absolute trust; For example; doctor giving an injection. At this level of trust, the client is just handing over the decision making to you.

2) Trusted advisor; A trusted advisor may be a accountant, a spiritual advisor, a lawyer. This is accepted as educated advice, The client feels your recommendation is for their benefit.

3) Friend; Most of us would rather buy from a friend. The client may not trust our judgment completely, but they know you are looking out for them. And they *want* to buy from you.

4) Friend of a friend; They know someone who bought from you. That's borrowed trust, and peer pressure. These people buy far more easily that at the Situational level.

5) Situational; You happen to call when they need what you have. You get the sale.

6) Brand trust; I sell Fords...you like Fords, or at least recognize the brand name Ford.

7) Spam; Beggars at airports. E-mail from strangers. Cold calls from untrained salespeople.

The higher the prospect sees you on this Level Of Trust, the easier it will be to get to see them and talk to them, and the easier it will be for them to follow your recommendation.

When cold calling, you are generally at level 6 or 7. Between the time you call, and the time you show up, you want to elevate them to a level 5 or 6. You can do that by sending them to a website, video, brochure, or a combination of these things.

Sales Prospecting By Claude Whitacre

After they become a client, and are familiar with your work, you want them at a 2 or 3. You get that mainly through superior customer service, and over delivering.

When seeing someone that was referred to you, being in the level 3 or 4 is desired. Most of those people will buy, provided you can give them a good reason, from their point of view.

I'd rather have 5 introductions than 50 referred leads, or a list of 1,000.
Let's pretend that you are a young man who is waiting to find a great girl to date. And, you love comic books.

You find that you have two choices that you can take advantage of this Saturday night.

1) You can go to a rally where there will be 2,000 people. A thousand people will be girls, but none of them know that you will be there...or even who you are.

2) There is a small gathering, where your friend says there is one girl who shares your love of comic books....and she is looking forward to meeting you. She has heard all about you. Her friends have told her that you are a good guy. You ask a few questions about this girl, and she sounds like your kind of girl.

You know she isn't dating anyone, and you hear that she's very cute and funny. Your friend will even point her out and introduce you.

So, where are you going on Saturday night? Are you going to go for a thousand girls, talk to them all, and hope you like one, and they like you?

Or are you going to see that one great girl that wants to meet you? Most will see the one great girl. In fact, they will drive further to meet one person that they are anxious to meet, than 1,000 that are just strangers.

That's the power of an introduced, qualified, referral.

Top sales people work by referrals, introductions, and sales to past customers.
After the first few years, when you have more than 100 high end clients that trust you, and will look forward to your call, your priorities change. You end up working mostly with past clients, their immediate family, and their referrals. You may do some networking, as I still do.

But if you can keep busy, just working with people who want to talk to you, your production will soar, because you aren't wasting time with unlikely buyers. Which leads me to.....

Sales Prospecting By Claude Whitacre

Cattle Rustlers VS Ranchers

By 1988, I had an office selling vacuum cleaners, and was doing quite well. I was satisfied with my life...until I met Julius Toth.

In the small town of Barberton, Ohio, Julius had a retail store selling vacuum cleaner...and was doing a million dollars a year in business, out of his small store. When I met him we immediately found out that we read the same sales books, listened to the same recordings, had the same outlook on many things, and we became close friends.

One morning we were sharing a breakfast. We would meet for breakfast once every week or so. We would trade sales stories, and motivate each other. I asked him one day what the difference was between what he did, and what I did. And this is what he said......

"Claude, let's pretend this is the old west. You are a cattle rustler. Every day, you go out looking for stray cattle that you can brand, and sell at auction. You make a good living, but your horse is tired, you have to sleep on the ground. Your horse has burrs under the saddle. You get cold at night..and every day, you have to start again, and repeat the same thing to make a living.

Me? I'm a rancher. I own a ranch. My cattle are cared for, fed well, and protected from the weather. My horses have horseshoes, are brushed every day, and don't freeze at night. When I need more cattle, I just breed them. Every day my ranch is worth more, and every day I have more cattle and more horses. I have a herd. You don't. I'm getting rich, you are not."

Imagine if someone said that to *you*.

This opened my eyes. I was knocking on doors until someone bought. Every day I repeated the same thing. Sure, I was making money, but I wasn't building a dependable, money making business. He was.

He was applying the idea to owning a high traffic retail store. Later, it dawned on me that it also applied to working by referrals. Want to build real wealth selling? Keep with one company, build a herd of clients, and take great care of them. The referrals you get from this hub of close clients will grow your business.

The 80/20 rule in referrals.
If you have been in sales for a while, you have heard of the "80/20 Rule". You know, 80% of your business will come from 20% or your customers. The figures may not be absolutely accurate, but the principle is true enough.

Sales Prospecting By Claude Whitacre

The truth is, some very good clients simply won't give you referrals. The truth is that the ones that do give you referrals, may give you bad referrals, that don't buy or are a headache. And some of your clients will give you an endless supply of highly qualified referrals that are eager to see you.

My own experience is about 90/10. That means that 10% of my clients (Those that have already bought) will give me 90% of the referrals that also buy.

After a few rounds of getting referrals and seeing them, you get a very good idea of who these "Best of the best" clients are. Treat them like gold because they are.

And, if I get referrals from a client, and they don't buy from me (maybe 3 in a row), I stop seeing that client's referrals. I also stop asking for referrals. This has only happened once or twice.

These referred, introduced leads from clients were closing at a higher than 90% rate. You'll very quickly discover how well you do with these referrals. And the clients that give me several sales when giving me referrals? I ask for more referrals. I have a few clients that have referred others to me, where they are the source of 40 sales or more.

Those people get gifts in appreciation. And I see to it that I refer business to *them*.

Should You Get Referrals From Every Customer?

You can. But I don't. In my retail store, they have to make a purchase for $300 or more, before I ask for referrals. And the reason it's that low, is because, in retail, I don't travel. All customers come to me. No travel time is wasted. When I sell my local online marketing program, they have to buy it before I ask for referrals. I only sell one package, and it's $6,000. I don't ask for referrals if they didn't buy.

If you ask for referrals from people who didn't buy, you will still make sales to those referrals. You'll just be selling at a lower rate than if they had bought. And if you ask for referrals from anyone who buys anything, you are spending an equal amount of time with referrals, that were told (by your customer) that they bought something inexpensive.

But what if you have multiple offers at a vast range of prices? Ask for referrals when customers buy your higher end offers. If you have a $100 product and a $5,000 product, concentrate on referrals from the $5,000 product. Because that's what the referred person will be thinking about, when you see them. And, that's the offer the referrer will be partly selling for you, before you get there.

Sales Prospecting By Claude Whitacre

Why we won't ask for referrals;
This is a painful subject, because I may take you out of your comfort zone. Most salespeople simply never ask for referrals. And most companies tell their salespeople, "Be sure to ask for referrals". But, they don't tell you how..because they don't know how. So, when I hear the reason that a salesperson doesn't ask for referrals, this is pretty much what I hear.

"I just don't like asking for referrals"
The reason you don't like asking for referrals, is that you don't know how to do it well. Maybe you think you are imposing on the customer. You aren't. Working with referrals is the professional way to prospect. Satisfied customers are very happy to refer you to others. It gives them a chance to brag about their deal, the service you provide, and how smart they were to invest with you. Have you recommended a restaurant to anyone you know? Giving referrals is...reviewing and recommending.

"I haven't done anything to deserve the referrals"
Maybe you haven't. Do you want to know how to deserve referrals? Give great service. Go the extra mile. Deliver more than promised. Now, you *deserve* referrals. And customers will be eager to give them.

Asking for referrals puts your client on a pedestal. You are letting her know that her recommendation means something.

"I don't know the right time to ask for referrals"
Here is when you ask for referrals; Right after the customers buys, before you leave. They are never going to be more excited about buying something, than at the moment they buy it. They are in *heat*. The customer just made a great discovery, your product. The discovery is what's exciting. When you find something exciting, don't you want to tell your friends about it? So do your clients. Ask for referrals when you give customer service (unless they are upset). Now, they will feel like they owe you, and will want to return the favor. They can show their gratitude by introducing you to their friends. And, right after you give your client a referral (if they are in business), or right after you recommend someone else to them. Do you want to know one reason the rich get richer? They are better *connected*. When you hear that someone is "well connected"? This is what that means. One business person referring their client to another business person. They refer each other to their friends. They are a valued resource, a "Center Of Influence".

People who connect suppliers to clients are at the hub of business activity. You want to be that person. And it also helps your client if they are that person too.

"Asking for referrals doesn't work."

No. Asking for referrals, the way you were *taught*, doesn't work. I've heard salespeople say that "Asking for referrals doesn't work" and I say, "No. You mean, the one time you asked for referrals, you didn't know what you were doing..and *that* attempt didn't work". I'm going to show you a method that works so well, an approach that is proven so effective that "not getting referrals" will have to be your choice.

"I need a reason for customers to give me referrals"

I think this is a legitimate concern. You can always bribe them with a gift. But I learned that there are better reasons to give referrals. Have you even referred a supplier to someone else? It makes you feel kind of important, doesn't it? You feel like you are helping two people, your supplier, and the friend you referred them to. When you buy something you love, don't you want your friends to know about it? Maybe you brag a little. But you feel good sharing what you discovered. By putting your friends in touch with a great resource, you are doing them a favor.

And you want to be a great resource for your clients.

"I don't want to ruin my relationship with the client"

Asking for referrals won't ruin your relationship. Do you want to ruin your relationship? Over promise, and under deliver. Miss deadlines, lie to them. But asking for referrals when you have earned them is just part of *strengthening* the relationship.

"I'll look like I need the business."

No you won't unless you do this completely wrong. Have you ever recommended a movie to a friend? Is it because you get a kickback from the movie theater? No! It's because you value their friendship. Have you ever seen a preview of a movie? At the end of a great preview, do you say, "They just showed this because they need me to buy a ticket"? No! Do you know who works almost exclusively by referrals? High end consultants, surgeons, attorneys, accountants, the wealthy. Do you know who never asks for referrals? The incompetent.

"They'll think I'm using our relationship to make money."

I hear this one fairly often. It really bothered me years ago, too. I thought that my customers would think ill of me, when I asked for referrals.

It never happened. It's a fear that exists only in a new salesperson's mind. Years ago, I asked a friend, who was a customer, if they thought it was wrong to ask for referrals. He laughed a little and said, "Are you joking? I like you and trust you. Who *else* would I want talking to my friends?". It really struck home.

Why people won't give you referrals
Yes, there are some people that simply do not want to give you referrals. This reaction doesn't happen often, but you should be prepared for it. Remember, your client sees everything from their point of view.

They don't want to give you referrals and introduce you because...

They aren't sure you can help their friend's specific problem.
Sometimes, the client sees you as the provider of a specific solution to a specific problem. If they can't think of anyone else with that specific problem they draw a blank when thinking about names to give you. They generally say, "I don't know anyone who needs a...". That's why you give a general profile of your best clients that is much broader than the specific reason your client bought.

They don't like you
I've worked with salespeople who sold in high volume, but they weren't likable. The product was needed so the prospect bought. But sending these guys to see your friends? Never. Have someone you trust go with you on an appointment to see if you are abrasive. If you smoke in someone's office or home, don't shower, or wear too much perfume, or chew tobacco in front of your clients....I may have found the problem.

They have had a bad experience giving referrals.
Many times this is the real answer. In fact, it's my assumed reason for not giving referrals. I simply ask them if they have had a bad experience in the past, giving referrals. Then I listen as they tell their tale of woe. I'll give it one more shot. Maybe say, "You should know by now, that I would never do anything to embarrass you. And I never give out confidential information. Can we talk about referrals on that basis, or would you rather not?"

Again, if you give fantastic service, and mention that you work by referral several times in your conversations, it will be very rare that you get an objection like this.

Sales Prospecting By Claude Whitacre

Actual customer responses;
I've had salespeople work for me most of my adult life. Once in a while I'll hear from a customer. Usually this is when I'm taking a service call, and the customer talks about the experience with the salesperson. Here is what some of them say.

"He wouldn't stop talking about himself, and I didn't want to put my friends through that".

"He stayed for two hours longer than he needed to. So I didn't want to do that to my friends".

"He smelled like smoke. We bought but my friends would hate me if I sent him to them".

If you are getting sales but not getting referrals, I promise, it's you. It's something you are doing that prevents you from getting referrals.

Your clients will only give you referrals for one reason; They *want* to.

Not getting referrals? Here's the cure; Incredible, proactive service.
This includes listening to the client when they are talking, treating them with respect, showing up on time, not overstaying your welcome, fulfilling your promises, and over delivering.

Remember, when they buy something that they really want...and feel like they got a great deal...and like the way you treated them..they will brag to their friends. You want to be introduced to the friends your client bragged to.

With superior service you'll deserve referrals, and your clients will want to give them to you. It makes them look good.

Clients want to help their friends, they want to help you, and they want to look good doing it.

You want the referral thinking, "This guy could be very valuable to me. I want to talk to him".

The client has already bragged about how you helped him, and your great service.

You will be the topic of conversation. That's the goal here.

The terrible way to ask for referrals, that you were probably taught...and why you stopped asking for referrals;
"Who do you know that could benefit from my product/service?" Here's why that question gets a terrible response. The client now has to imagine everyone they know. This image is a massive blur in their mind. And to them it will take time to sort it out.

Sales Prospecting By Claude Whitacre

So they just say, "I'll get back to you on that", or "I can't think of anyone right now".

"Who do you know who might be interested in what I sell?" How the heck is your client going to know who's interested in what you sell? The reason they give you referrals is because you will meet their friend, and then you'll find out if the friend wants what you sell, or not. The client referral is for a meeting, not necessarily for a sale. Although, if the client has already talked to the referral about your service, a sale is far more likely.

"Who do you know that is a home owner/business owner/friend/relative/lawyer/doctor?" This is a little better. Decades ago, when I sold life insurance we used a flip book that asked these questions to trigger referral names. But a good referral is determined by far more than what they do for a living. We will be talking about the Best Client Profile a little later.

Referring because of you or because of your offer.

Your client will probably talk to the referral about your offer. That's a good thing. The referral is now used to the idea that what you sell is popular, and their friend believes in it.

But I'm more interested in getting referrals that will be told about the experience of meeting me, and what they will learn.

That's "Selling the appointment", not the product.

I want the client saying things like, "Claude showed us several options to increase our sales. He knows his stuff, and we learned quite a lot just from the meeting. Sure, we decided to do business with him, but the meeting itself was productive. You need to meet him."

The way you accomplish that is by making your meeting with your future client informative and productive. This is covered in more detail in my book One Call Closing.

I want people to be glad they met me, whether they buy or not. That paves the way for an abundance of referrals. It also causes the focus of a discussion, between your client and his friends to include other reasons to meet you besides just buying your product.

To give a ten second explanation on how I accomplish this I show options to solve problems (In the actual presentation), and give them everything they need to know about their options. Although I'm really giving useful information another benefit to explaining options is to give the prospect the feeling that they have shopped around and compared options. So there is less need for another meeting. I close in one call.

Sales Prospecting By Claude Whitacre

Asking everyone for referrals.

The problem with asking non-clients for referrals, is that they have so little to tell the referral before you meet the referral. What can they say, "He's a nice guy, please talk to him"?

The exception is the "Center of Influence". These are typically heads of organizations, owners of companies, people who are very involved in civic affairs. These are people that will open doors for you.

Asking non buyers for referrals.

This means asking a person that you have presented to, and didn't buy, for referrals.

First, let me say, that if you give gifts for presentations, you will eventually sell a person that was referred by a non-buyer. It does happen. But these referrals from non-buyers, are not as prepared to buy as even a cold call prospect.

Think about this; If you watched a movie and didn't like it would you give it a good recommendation? No. You're asking for referrals, from someone that didn't want your service enough to buy it. What are they going to tell their referrals? It will not be, "I was a fool for not buying this, you should buy it". It will be something like, "It wasn't for me, it was too expensive, But, I promised I'd give the guy some referrals. Do what you want".

After a decade of testing, I just became convinced that it's very difficult to get good referrals from people who didn't buy. People who don't buy, tend to give you names of people who also don't buy. Sure, you will sell a few. But this book is about finding the people that are highly likely to buy when you meet them. And asking for referrals from people who said "No" to your offer, isn't the way. This is also one of the main reasons salespeople stop asking for referrals. They are asking the wrong people.

Common Objections To Giving You Referrals

"Let me think about some people, and I'll get back to you"
This doesn't feel like an objection, but it is. It's a way to get out of giving you referrals. In the rare event that I hear this I just say, "Why don't we just take a minute to describe who an ideal referral is. OK?". The client should have a very clear idea of who you want to talk to, before you even ask. This is the Best Client Profile we will be talking about. If you hear this objection repeated, then I would back off. They just don't want to give you a referral now. I may ask, "Why don't we let that simmer for awhile. Names will come to you after you tell your friends about your experience with our product. Is it OK to talk about this in a few months?" And, I do call back.

If they *still* say (which has never happened to me), "I'll call you with names if I think of any", that means to not bring it up again, forever.

"If I hear of anyone who needs your service, I'll tell them about you"

If they say that as you are asking about referrals, you have done something wrong, or they just really don't want to give you referrals. If they say this when we haven't talked about referrals, I'll ask them, "Why don't we take a minute to describe what an ideal referral is. OK?"

If they say this when I'm asking for referrals, I say, "I appreciate that. Let's take a minute to talk about who makes the best referral, OK?", and I just go back into describing my Clint Profile.

"I will tell everyone I know all about you"

No, they won't. It's a nice way of saying, "I like you, but I'm not going to take the time to refer you". It's the same as saying, "You're a great salesman", as you are walking out the door. The client is trying to be polite. Maybe they don't know what else to say. I just say, "Well, no need to tell everyone. Let's take just a minute to talk about who makes a great referral, and narrow it down a bit, OK?"

"It's illegal for me to give you referrals"

I suppose that this is possible, although I've never seen a law against it. It may be company policy. Although it's far more likely that the policy is against receiving a gift for giving a referral. You are more likely to hear this in the financial sales arena.

"Not a problem. I should have been more clear. Who do you know *outside your industry*, personal friends in other businesses, who would benefit from meeting me?"

Really, it's never illegal to give referrals. It may be illegal to get *paid* for referrals (in just a few industries) but it's never illegal to refer you to someone they know. But there are still some people who believe this. And convincing them otherwise is a long unwelcome process.

And, I never ask for referrals after a second stall. It doesn't matter what their reason is.

"I don't like sending salespeople after my friends. Someone sent a salesman after me, and I didn't appreciate it"

If you hear anything like this, there has been a real breakdown in the selling process. They should never see you as someone they are "unloading" on their friends.

Sales Prospecting By Claude Whitacre

You can say;
"That isn't how you think of me, and that's not how your friend will think of me. If you believe that I can add value to your friend's business...then help us meet. They will see it as a favor, just as you have"

Your referral source must embrace the fact that she is doing her friend a favor, by introducing you to them. There is no other way this works. It cannot be thought of as a favor to *you*.

"I can't think of anyone"
"I get that at first from nearly all my best referral sources. Let's talk about what a great referral looks like....and .the names will flow. OK?"

"I don't know if Bill is interested"
"I know. I'm just looking for an introduction, and Bill can decide where it goes from there. OK?"

"My friends already have someone taking care of this"
"I know. Everyone I talk to already has someone. That just means that they already understand the need for what I do. You always benefit from having more than one option, when using suppliers. I just want to be introduced to them, and share some information about what we can do. It's always better to have more than one vendor. Does that make sense?"

The trap of giving you names just so you'll stop asking.

I've only had this experience a few times. You get referrals, you start calling them, and you realize that the referrer hasn't really talked to them. Or you find out that the referrals are not as the client described. Or you find out that they aren't really interested in talking to you.

I once had a client that was very influential in town. He gave me ten referrals, that he said he talked to, and were waiting to see me. He was telling the truth about them being willing to see me. But on every appointment, the prospect would do something like insist on watching TV while they were talking to me. One woman sat at her desk and *knitted*, while I was presenting. She didn't look at me once. One referral wouldn't sit in the same room as me. She was washing dishes in the kitchen (Or some other chore). This appointment was in her home. She just kept saying, "I can hear you just fine. Keep talking".

I went on four or five of these nightmarish appointments, before I got the message. The client thought it would be funny to put me through the ringer. I have no idea why. I talked to him years later, and he told me what he did. He thought it was a great joke, that I should find hilarious. I didn't.

Sales Prospecting By Claude Whitacre

Clients "returning the favor" for someone who referred them.
I actually ask for these, and make a joke about it. In fact, I make a point of asking for the names of someone who referred a salesman to them, that they bought from. But I want to make it clear that I only want the name if they *bought* from the salesperson. Buyers "returning the favor" almost always buy. I don't remember ever *not* selling one of these referrals. You probably couldn't make a living, just seeing these "return the favor" referrals, but it sure helps.

Unsolicited referrals "You should call my uncle"
Sometimes you'll get a call out of the blue. "Yeah, you should talk to Bob, over at ACME Tire. He sure needs what you have". Don't just call. Ask your client, why they think Bob is a good prospect. Ask if they talked to Bob. Ask what Bob said in return. Later in this book, we will talk a little about contacting non introduced referrals. My experience is that they are usually not good leads, unless Bob really wants to talk to me. However, I always thank the referral source.

www.ClaudeWhitacre.com

"The best way to guarantee that you get referrals, is to give them"

-Claude

www.ClaudeWhitacre.com

The One Call Closer's Referral Selling Method

The overriding thought when working by referrals, is that the client should expect to give them to you. You should deserve them. The client should talk to others about your offer and you personally, and the referrals should be anticipating your call.

Whew! So that's selling by referrals, in a nutshell.

The entire approach with The One Call Closer's Referral Selling Method breaks down into five components…

Sales Prospecting By Claude Whitacre

- Creating a Best Client Profile.
- Preparing the client to welcome the idea of giving you referrals
- Getting the referrals and qualifying them
- Having the client introduce you to the referral, either in person or by phone.
- Calling the referrals to set the appointment

Your Best Client Profile.

As we mentioned before in the 80/20 Rule. 80% of your business comes from 20% of your clients. And 80% of your referrals will come from 20% of your client. There will be some overlap between these two groups, but they are separate groups.

Why have a Best Client Profile?
I had heard about this when reading about direct mail marketing for years. It was under different names, but the meaning was the same. Picture who your desired customer is, and direct your presentation to *that person*.

I finally decided to try this for my own sales, and came up with an interesting mix. We are talking about the top 20% that gives you most of your business. That's who we are going to profile.

If you think about your best customers, you'll find they have commonalities that they share.

Maybe not all of them, but most of them. For example, in my local online marketing service, I found that my best clients were generally like this;

Brick and mortar business owners

- Customers came to them, or their service area was very local
- Average sales ticket of $500 or more.
- They sold something specific. No retail stores that offered hundreds of product categories.
- The owner answered the phone, or would come to the phone, no gatekeepers.
- No committees, the owner was the decision maker.
- They advertised their business with conventional advertising
- They at least had a website already.

I was pretty inflexible on this list. Whether I was cold calling or asking for referrals I was more inflexible with referrals.

When I was selling to consumers in their home, the list was different.

1) Homeowner

2) At least one full time job between the husband and wife

Sales Prospecting By Claude Whitacre

3) If a couple, both must be present for the presentation

4) If it was a referral, it was a huge plus if they had bought from an in home salesperson before, and gave that person referrals...who, in turn, bought. We'll talk about that later, when we discuss the "Follow the salesperson" strategy.

Qualifications1-3 were mandatory. If the referrals were renters, the chance of a sale was slightly less, but the chance of getting them financed, was *far* less. The people who didn't work full time would be impossible to get financed, and they would invariably say, "Well, when I get a full time job, I'm going to get one of these". When both spouses weren't present, that practically guaranteed a sale wasn't going to happen. Any one of these three was enough to disqualify the prospect. No exceptions. Almost every exception I made turned into a wasted effort.

A little later you will read the list of questions I ask my client about the referrals they give me. That list is longer than the list above. There are some things I would like to know, and are useful when selling. These lists contain things I need to know before I'll take the time to present them to a referral.

Another reason for a Best Client Profile

The average person knows 250 people well enough to invite to a wedding. But you don't want to see all those 250. You want to see the three or four that are highly qualified to buy your offer. That's why you build a Best Client Profile. You want to shrink the universe that your client has to look at. And you want to shrink it in the direction of your Ideal Client Profile.

When I'm about to ask for referrals, I'll take 30 seconds to tell the client what I'm looking for.

This will eliminate leads that are completely wrong for my offer. It will also trigger ideas for names that the client may not have thought of.

How I segue into the "Best Client Profile" discussion.

"Here are the types of people that will appreciate the introduction"

"People who will be the most grateful for being introduced to me are..."

Preparing the client to welcome and anticipate the request for referrals.

Sprinkled in your presentation are several things you can say that present the idea of referrals as a normal part of the discussion.

Sales Prospecting By Claude Whitacre

You want to avoid the idea that you are asking for a favor, or that they are doing you a favor. You want to position the referral as a favor the client is doing for their friend, and as a way to look like a hero to their friends.

Positioning referrals as the central way you do business.

"Nearly all of my clients come from referrals from other happy clients, that want to help their friends. I've found that "word of mouth" is the best way to advertise. So I want to give the kind of service you can't help but tell your friends about".

It's useful to include the idea that you buy through referral, too. Selling by referrals is the *preferred way* for anyone to do business. That's the message here.

"I was referred to see a guy about..." or, "I had a client that was referred by his___ and here's what happened..." Only insert a couple of times in the presentation, or the technique will become noticeable.

Here's a way to cement the idea that referrals are the way to buy and sell, and to promote the idea that reviews and recommendations are what drive the economy.

"My clients have told me that they would rather be referred by their trusted friends than just cold called".

Yes, I *do* say that, even if I cold called this prospect. I want to set up the idea that referrals are the preferred method of selling by all involved parties. Even when I'm on an appointment that I got from cold calling one of the first things I'll say at the appointment is, "I work mostly by referral".

Position referrals as something you will do *for* them and their friends.

"Your opinion means a lot to me. I'd be happy to talk to your friends based on your recommendation". This also builds up the client as someone who's recommendation is taken seriously. You can also say;

"I'm glad you see the value in this. You know, I'm never too busy to help your friends by letting them know about this. I'll make every effort to fit them in my schedule.."

And, "I'm building a business based on providing so much value to my clients, they naturally want to tell others about me. Make sense?"

The best way to bring up referrals to get the ball rolling.

"How will I know if someone is a good referral for you?". Of course, this will only work in business sales. The way to make this work even better is to either give them a referral right then, or introduce them later to someone who can buy from them. The best way to ensure that you *get* referrals and introductions, is to *give* referrals and introductions.

The segue to asking for referrals.

This is the moment when you are going to ask for referrals. I do this at the conclusion of the sale. Right after they have signed any paperwork, and the sale is essentially done.

"Would it be OK if we took a minute to think of a few people who *you think should at least know about this/the work I do/this service*?"

Or

"Would it be OK if we took a minute to think of a few people *you would like to help, and would benefit from this information*?"

Either of these questions puts the client in the position of *helping their friends* by giving you as a resource.

I ask these questions in a way that shows the client that they are questions I ask every day to everyone who buys from me. And they are. In no way does the client ever perceive that this is as important to me as the fact that they bought from me. I'm very relaxed, and ....it's very much like, "this is no big deal. Everyone gives me referrals".

The power of "By Referral Only".
On one of my business cards, it has written in bold "By Referral Only". Why? Because now the prospect is in a select group.

Have you ever seen a line outside a nightclub? One of the reasons everyone wants to get in there...is because they know it's hard to get in the nightclub. People want what's hard to get.

I say, "I only work by referral", and my card says "By Referral Only" to give the following impressions;

1) I don't need to ask people to buy from me, they are looking for me.

2) Not everyone can get to me. Someone has to refer you to me.

3) If I work with you, it's because you are special.

4) If I see you, it's because the person who referred you *did you a favor*.

Of course, when I'm cold calling I don't say that I only work by referrals. But sometimes I say, "I normally work only by referral. But your company interests me, and I want to meet you". Try saying "No" to *that*.

When to ask for referrals

Getting Referrals At The Point Of Sale. You'll be gathering referrals as time passes too. But I strongly suggest that you also get referrals from the initial meeting.

This is before the client sees results from your sale. It's based on the information you provided, and the excitement of a new purchase. The customer is "in heat" at that moment, and is highly likely to be willing to give you referrals.

Getting referrals when the client calls you or needs service. After you have had a client for a few months they have told several people the story of your presentation and what you did for them. By this time your client has either complained about the experience, or bragged about it. You want to see the people he bragged to. If he contacts them for you, they are almost certain to buy from you, as long as the offer applies to them.

Getting referrals when they just gave you a referral. I know this may sound strange, but one of the best times to ask for a referral is when they just gave you one. You are already on the phone with them. I've found that the client usually has a couple more people that they have talk to about your product or you.

Getting referrals right after you gave them a referral. I can't stress this enough, the best way to guarantee a steady supply of qualified referrals is to give a referral to your client. This strengthens the relationship and shows that you care about their business. When you are on the phone with them, giving your referral, it's the perfect time to mention that you would see a friend of theirs.

Not referrals...Introductions. Here's how the "getting referrals" process works for most salespeople. They ask for a few referrals and the customers says, "I can't think of anyone today". After a few attempts the salesperson determines that, "Nobody gives referrals anymore".

Or

The salesperson asks for referrals, and get a list of referrals.

Sales Prospecting By Claude Whitacre

Then the salesperson calls them, and the people act like they don't know your client, or they say, "He never mentioned this to me. Is this a scam?" Or, "I'll talk to Bob (your client) first to see what he says about you".

In all situations, the salesperson finds that selling by referral is simply not for them.

Well, there is one missing ingredient that makes all the difference... The Introduction.

If the client talks to the referral before you call them, and the referral agrees to talk to you, you are in a *far* stronger position to sell that referral. This idea makes me so much money that I won't call a referral unless the customer has called ahead of me, and introduced me, and the prospect has agreed to talk to me.

Why is it so important that your client talk to the referral first? Because 80% of the selling is done *there*. I'm not kidding.

Having the client *introduce* me to the referral, is the single most important part of selling by referrals.

First of all, if the referral tells the client that they will talk to you, the odds that they will *take your call* just shot up to about 100%.

The odds that the referral will *see* you, just shot up to about 95%.

And, in my experience, the odds that they will buy from you on your first call just shot up to about 80%. Your odds will differ, but, the numbers for "taking your call" and "seeing you" are pretty accurate for everyone.

And why are they far more likely to buy from you on the first call? Because the recommendation from a trusted friend...that also bought from you...is enough to give most people enough confidence in your offer, and enough willingness to trust you....to buy.

And if the referral knows four or five people, all of whom bought from you, the sale is almost a forgone conclusion, because of perceived peer pressure. That's why referrals in niches are so powerful. They tend to know each other, and what each of the group is buying.

So, I get the referral names, then ask for some qualifying information for each name, and then ask to be introduced. But the introduction is the most important part.

Sales Prospecting By Claude Whitacre

Getting the names, and qualifying.
When I start asking for names, I just use a yellow legal pad. At first, I just want the names. After I get four or five names I start asking questions about the referrals to find out more about them, and qualify them, or unqualify them. I used to use a form that had spaces for answers to every question. But if the client saw the form, it immediately looked like a lot of work to fill it all out. Now I just ask for the names, write them down, and then go back and ask questions about each name.

Getting the names. This is a list of questions I ask to put the picture of a few friends in front of the client's mind. It makes these choices easier for the client to see.

Business sales:

"Who have you told about the service we provide you?"

These are the people that the client has bragged to about you and your service. These names are of the highest quality, usually. I like these names because it's far easier to get an appointment with them. I also ask, "What did they say?", because that will tell me if the referral will be likely to buy from me.

126

"Who is also in your business that you think should have this information?"

I actually say, "Who is also in your business, *but not in your area*, that you think should have this information?", because I sell an area exclusive service. One per town. Most business owners are not good friends with local competitors. But they have lots of close friends in their business that they see at conventions and industry events. If you have to travel to meet the prospect you might want to put a limit on the distance. Limit it to the same county, or the same state, for example. I can sell my service completely over the phone, but it's not my preferred method.

"Who do you know well that is in a different business than yours, and local?"

Most businesspeople have friends in different businesses in their same town. If you want to stay local, this is a great question to ask. These names may also be some of the, "Who did you tell about this?" names.

"What about members of any local organizations you belong to?"

This brings up new names of people the client knows in the Chamber of Commerce, Kiwanis, or any other local organization.

Sales Prospecting By Claude Whitacre

Make sure that the client knows them well. You don't want a roster of 100 members of an organization. When you get to the part where you ask to be introduced a long list will make the client balk at introducing you to so many. That's why I keep each list of referrals to 4 or 5 names. Sometimes, all the names I need are from asking, "Who did you tell about this?".

"How about someone who gave you as a referral, and you bought?"

This is actually a name I want. I ask the question with a smile on my face, because it may be a little game the clients play with each other. Some people send salespeople to each other as a form of "Tag!. You're it!". These people will nearly always see you, and if your offer applies to them at all...they will buy from you. I do not want the name of someone you send salespeople to..that never buys. These are two completely different groups, with a different relationship.

That's why I say, "...and you bought".

"How about someone you have referred other suppliers to, that has bought?"

This is a referral that the client has given to someone else already, and they bought. You are now literally repeating the process.

Again, they almost always will see you, and they will almost always buy. I talk about this more in the section on the "Follow the salesman" strategy. This single strategy *alone* gave me a great income for almost a year.

"What about reps you buy from?"

Your offer may not apply to this approach. But if you sell something that virtually anyone in business can use this will get you people that will see you easily. And there is a slight obligation for them to buy, to keep rapport with their customer, your client.

"What about business customers that could benefit from this information?"

Again, this may not apply. Would some of your client's customer base benefit from what you offer? We already know that the person likes and trusts your client, and is used to spending money on his recommendation. A good source if it applies to your offer.

Consumer sales;

I'm going to assume, if you are selling a consumer product, that you simply want to see qualified people who can buy, if they decide to.

Sales Prospecting By Claude Whitacre

When I was selling high end vacuum cleaners in people's homes, this is the list of people I asked for. Again, just four or five names at a time.

Who do you ask for?

Close friends, parents, brothers, sisters, kids, co-workers or friends at church. These are the natural lists of names. These people will probably see you because the relationship they have with your customer is strong.

I ask for these names *first*.

People they have referred a salesman to, in the past, that bought. This is the single best referral you can get. These prospects have proven that they will talk to a salesperson, and will buy from them on the first call. Again, we will cover this more in the section on "Follow the salesman".

And, like the business clients, I ask for the people that sent a salesperson to talk to the client, in the past, and they bought from that salesperson. Again, you can't get a stronger lead.

And, like the business clients, I'll ask, "Who did you already talk to about this?". Why? Because they bragged about their new product. They told the price, in almost every case.

If you get to see these people, a sale is almost assured.

Again, I stop asking for names after I get four or five referrals. If the name is unqualified (we are getting to that now), then I replace it with another name, and ask questions about *that* person.

Qualifying the referrals as you receive them.
After I get a list of several names, never more than ten, I start asking questions about the names I was given. Some of these questions are just to help me sell, but a few will disqualify the referral right away.

It's important to ask these questions *before* you ask for an introduction. You don't want to be talking to someone who would make a bad client, or couldn't buy..and waste your time, and create bad feedback to your referrer. And you don't want the client to introduce you, and then you discover that this is an unqualified lead.

Qualifying questions to ask in business sales;

"How do you know them?" I want the client to really know the referral. I don't want a list of names. I want a list of close relationships. No membership lists, no mailing lists. I want friends that the client can call up and always talk to.

Sales Prospecting By Claude Whitacre

If the client calls the referral, and the referral tells the receptionist, "Take a message", that's bad. I want the names of *friends*. And write down the specific answer. If the client says, "He's my brother-in-law" don't write down "relative". You may have to remind the referral how they know the client when you call.

"What type of business do they have?" This can also be, "What kind of work do they do?". You want to verify that the prospect is working, and if she is in the same business as the client.

"How long have they been in business?" I just need a rough estimate. It also tells me if this is the person who started the business, or a second generation owner. In fact, often I'll just ask that.

"Employees? How many?" If it applies to your offer, ask. I ask because it also lets me know how easy it will be to talk to the referral and how busy she may be.

"Sole owner, or is there a partner?" If it's a partner, and I need them to be there for the appointment, now it's the time to find out if a partner exists.

"Why do you think they would benefit from talking to me?" I ask them this in every business sale. I want the client to sell me a little on the referral as a prospect. I just write down whatever they tell me.

"Have you referred them before? Have they referred you before?" This is a far more important question than it sounds. If I don't already know that this referral is already part of a referral chain, I want to know now. And then I always ask, "Did they buy?" or, "Did you buy?" If there was a sale, my odds of making a sale just shot through the roof. If there was no sale that doesn't mean it's a bad referral, but, then I'll ask, "Why do you think a sale didn't happen?". The answer to *that* question will tell me if I still want to see this referral.

"If you were me, who would you want to see first? And Why?" This answer may surprise you. Sometimes there won't be an answer. But you may hear, "See Bob, he told me that he wanted to talk to you about buying your service". I've heard that same thing. And, I wouldn't have been told if I didn't ask.

"Is there anyone I should save to call later? Why?" Did Joe just get a divorce? Is Cindy going bankrupt? Is there a merger? Is someone moving? This is when you want to find out.

Sales Prospecting By Claude Whitacre

You don't want to find out at the appointment.

And those are the questions I ask. Of course, then I get the phone number. The direct number, if possible. The town too. But I don't need to know the exact address until I have an appointment.

Qualifying questions to ask in consumer sales:

"Employment? how long?" This is a credit question. It also shows if they just got a job. When I was selling in people's homes, it was my first question.

"Are they homeowners or renters?" I ask because of credit. It's much easier to get a homeowner financed. Even if I've told the client earlier that I want homeowners as referrals, I still ask. Sometimes it slips their minds.

"Married? Kids?" For me, I just wanted to know if they were married, because I want both of them to be there. In fact, I won't run the appointment if the husband or wife are alone. If they have kids is just a question that was good to know. People with kids at home tended to buy just a little easier.

"Have you told them about me?" If they have told the referral about you, so much the better. The price was probably discussed, too. If this person will see you they will almost certainly buy. You may have already noted this, on your list of names.

"What have they bought from an in home salesperson?" This is specific to in-home sales. If they have bought from an in-home salesperson before the odds are far greater that they will buy from you, too. Again, you may already have his information. But I always ask, if I don't know the answer.

"Have you referred them before? Have they referred you before?" Again, two sides of the same coin. These "referral sold prospects" are far easier to see, and far easier to sell. And I want to know if the prospect *bought*. That's even more *important*. If someone says, "Yeah we've sent 7 salespeople to see old Jack, and he never buys from any of them", I don't want to see Jack. I'm not in this business for the challenge. I want easy sales. So I stick to the methods that get me easy sales.

"Who would you call first, and why?" "Who should I wait to see later, and why?" Like the business sale, I just want to know if there is something I missed.

Sales Prospecting By Claude Whitacre

If Aunt Lucy just won the lottery, and is buying everything in sight, I want to know. Wouldn't you? If Nephew Bobby is going to prison in a week, I don't want to go see Nephew Bobby.

Then I get the phone number, and the town they live in. I can get the exact address later.

You may also ask for specific criteria. For example, if you sell a product that helps with allergies, you should ask if the referral has allergies. The client may, or may not know that. If you sell security equipment for homes, you could ask, "Have you ever suffered a burglary in your home?".

It's just as easy to get an ideal referral as a bad one.
The reason we ask all these questions is that the client is going to be asked to contact the referrals for us. And it's just as easy for the client to call a qualified referral, as an unqualified one.

The client doesn't know who you want to talk to until you tell them. They also don't know what specific things you are looking for unless you tell them.

Bringing up the idea of introducing you to the referral.

Here is why you only want to get four or five referrals at a time. You are going to ask the client to contact each one of your qualified referrals, by phone, and ask if they will see you for an appointment. There are several points in that last sentence.

You are asking the client to call, on the phone, the referral. You are not asking them to use the client's name, and call the referrals yourself. You are not asking the client to e-mail the referral. You want the client to call the referral on the phone and talk to the referral. You don't want the client asking the secretary to make the calls for him. And, you don't want the client just leaving a message with a gatekeeper. You want the client to talk to the actual referral.

You are also asking the client to ask if the referral will see you, in person, for an appointment. You are not asking if it's Ok to e-mail the referral. You are not asking if you can mail the referral literature. You are specifically asking the client to call the referral, on the phone, and ask them if they will talk to you, in person, by appointment. You need to memorize this last sentence.

Sales Prospecting By Claude Whitacre

No other arrangement will come close to being as effective as a personal introduction, by phone, with permission to call the referral to arrange an appointment.

I know I went a little overboard on the last two paragraphs, but it's for a good reason. This is not a place to shortcut. Any change to the process, and it will not work.

Whenever I hear salespeople tell me that they have tried his method, and it didn't work...it's always because they didn't get the client to call, by phone, the referral and get permission for you to see the referral in person, by appointment. This is also where most salespeople mess this up. It just feels like too much work, and so they settle for, "I'll give you his e-mail address, and you can mention that you know me". If that happens, you are wasting your time.

Here is what I ask after I get the first names on the list;

"Bob, your friends would *much* prefer hearing from you, before they hear from me. They are going to want to know why you think they should take my call, and why they should see me. Let's come up with an introduction that you find comfortable, OK?"

And now, you have a choice. You can have the client call a couple of the referrals in front of you, or you can ask the client to call the referrals over the next couple of days and you will call him back. Personally, I usually get the calls done in the office while I'm there. Why? Because many business owners screen their calls with "Caller ID". And, they will take the friend's call, while my call would go to Voicemail.

Another segue you can use is, "My clients all tell me that they would far prefer to be introduced, by a respected friend that they know well, than to be cold called. Does that make sense?"

And then you can say, "What I would like you to do is call Mike (the first one on the list) and tell him that you are here with me, and that he should see me...whether he ends up buying from me or not. He should still meet me to evaluate what we have to offer. Will you do that for me now?"

Nowadays, here is exactly what I say and do; The next two paragraphs are almost verbatim what you read in my book **"Selling Local Advertising"**. It's exactly what I say. I just had it included in both books.

Sales Prospecting By Claude Whitacre

"The best referral you gave me is Joe. Is Joe at his business right now? May I borrow your phone for a second?" (Or, "May I call him right now, in front of you?") The only reason you want to use the client's phone, is that the person you call may have Caller ID. If you call from your phone, they may not pick up the phone. But if you call from the client's phone... they will.

It isn't necessary to use the client's phone, but you'll get through more often. And you call Joe. Right there, in front of Bill. Do it. You'll get an entirely different reaction from Joe than if you waited and called by yourself.

If you call & get a gatekeeper (secretary, assistant, mother) hand the phone to Bill and have him ask for Joe. If you get Joe, just say, *"Hi, this is Claude Whitacre with Local Profit Geyser. I'm sitting here with your friend Bill.. Say 'Hi' Bill (Bill says 'Hi' into the phone). Anyway, I've done some work with Bill to take advantage of online traffic and make it more profitable (or whatever benefit Bill got from you). I have no way of knowing if I can really be of service to you... but I promised Bill that I would at least show you what we do. Would you have 15 minutes today or tomorrow, that I can stop by, and introduce myself? I promise not to take longer than that."*

This referral script is so effective that I've had several clients ask me to teach it to their reps.... after I called the prospect from their office.

You have to say, "I promised Bill that I would at least *show* you what we do.". Not, "*Tell* you what we do" but, "*Show* you what we do". And the fact that you promised Bill? Now Joe has to say, "OK, you can come on over tomorrow at 2PM" or he's saying "No" to Bill. See that? He isn't saying "No" to you, he's saying "No" to Bill, your client.

Sure, it's slightly nervy. And it isn't for everyone. If you have any names that they gave you, because these referrals have sent sales reps to each other in the past, now's the time to "return the favor". These are the first names to call, and, anyone that has been told about me, and showed interest. They should be called right from the office. It's an effortless call that the client will nearly always make. Those calls are actually fun for the client. He gets to show off a little.

If you feel very uncomfortable asking your client to call the referral right there in front of you, you can ask them to talk to the referral after you leave. If the client is going to make the calls I limit the number of calls to four. The four best referrals.

Sales Prospecting By Claude Whitacre

I say, "To make it easier on your friends, would you do them a favor and call these four people. Make sure they know that you recommended they take my call...and that you suggested they see me for a short appointment?"

Sometimes the client immediately gets everything you are trying to do. They usually just smile, and get on the phone while you are sitting there. Sometimes you have to explain, three or four times, exactly what you want. If they aren't real busy, they may make one call for you, while you are there. If they are pressed for time (or just want to get to other things), ask them to call these four friends and to make the introduction on your behalf.

If they say they will call these referrals make sure you let them know that you will be calling them back in a day or two to see who they talked to.

I generally wait two business days, and call the client back. "Hello Bob, Claude here. Did you get a chance to talk to one or two of the referrals we discussed?" I'm going to call Bob back maybe two more times, every couple of days. If I feel that he's cooling off to the idea, I may say,

"Why don't we just try one referral. Could you call John Jones right now, while this is in front of you? I can call you back in 15 minutes or so."

Here are my results when asking for the introductions;

40% make the calls (at least one) while I'm sitting in their office. Some of these referrals actually told the client that they wanted to see me already, or at least the client told them about me, and this process becomes almost effortless.

45% will call all of the referrals in the next couple of days, and pave the way for me.

15% just become mysteriously unavailable when I call their office. Those people get an e-mail from me thanking them for the referrals, and letting them know that I'll get in touch when I have the results of my calls. And those referrals, I just call on my own.

These referrals are part of the system, and do get called....eventually But they are low on my list.

The referrals that the client actually talks to, and paves the way for me? Those are the people I concentrate on. The "I'll contact them on my own" referrals get called just ahead of the cold calls. Cold calls get called last, when I've run out of referrals for that day.

Giving results to referrer. Keep them in the loop.
You need to tell the client the results of every call. You are only calling a small number of referrals per client, so it's not much of an effort to keep the client informed. And that's the least you can do. Always keep it positive. If you get a sale just say, "I was able to help Bill, and I wouldn't have been able to meet with him without you. Thank you."

If you get an appointment, but no sale, just call and say, "I wanted to thank you for the introduction. The meeting went well, and I can see why you guys are friends. We shared some ideas that will help both of us in our businesses. Hopefully, he and I will be able to work together down the road".

If an appointment falls through, say, "We played tag for awhile. But our paths never crossed. I just wanted to thank you for the effort you put into introducing us".

And, you know the best time to ask for more referrals is right then, on that call.

Your client can see that you appreciate the introductions, and that the referrals are getting something out of the meetings. Remember, you still have more referrals that you have qualified. The client can call them now, if they like.

Speed is important here. A week or two after the introduction is made, the referral may forget who you are, or why you are calling.

Referral Incest

When you start seeing lots of referrals, and they are in the same niche or the same town you will begin to see that you are getting some of the same referral names. For example, I was selling my local online marketing service to owners of vacuum cleaner specialty stores. Eventually, they began to give me names that I had already seen. You'll see this in even larger groups, like trade associations.

What I do then is ask the client for referrals who are not in the same business. Maybe an owner of a Karate studio gives me a couple of referrals of other Karate studio owners he knows. But I'll also want to get the name of his printer or someone else he works closely with. That way, the referrals become more diverse, and still fit your "Client Profile"

Of course, if you are in a business that only sells to dentists, then you will diversify the area served, but not the niche.

Referral Phone Scripts When Calling The Referral

If the prospect is very local;

"Hello, Bill? This is Claude Whitacre. I'm the owner of Local Profit Geyser, and I believe Paul Jones told you a little about me? (Yes) Well, Paul spoke very highly of you, and he asked me to give you a call. I promised Paul that I would stop by, and show you the kind of work I do, so you can decide for yourself if it applies to your business. Fair enough?"

If the prospect is within travel distance but not 10 minutes away, it is essentially the same conversation, but I want to qualify them more before I drive for an hour.

"Hello, Bill? This is Claude Whitacre. I'm the owner of Local Profit Geyser, and I believe Paul Jones told you a little about me? (Yes) Well, Paul spoke very highly of you, and he asked me to give you a call. I promised Paul that I would visit with you, and tell you a little about what I do? Do you have a minute?"

And then I ask them a few qualifying questions about their business. I just want to make sure they fit my Client Profile. They almost always do.

"Well, it sounds like we should talk further. How about tomorrow at 3PM. Is that a good time, or should we shift it around a little?"

Believe me, they have already decided if they will see you. This is just so they can hear your voice and let them know that you are coming. It's important that you call (and not just show up), but don't spend time talking about your product. You don't need to talk them into seeing you. I've seen lots of salespeople talk introduced prospects *out* of seeing them.

Objections to an appointment, when you call them to set the time.
Objections to an appointment with a qualified referral are different than objections with a cold call. I mean they are treated differently. On a cold call I can just go to the next call. But, there has been some investment in getting these referrals. There has been an investment of effort by your client in paving the way for your appointment.

These aren't really objections. The referral will think of a reason why they don't need to talk to you, or see you until later...like ten years later.

Keep this in mind. You can't let this turn into, "I'm trying to make an appointment with you". It has to remain, "Bob made me promise to see you in person, and you told Bob that you would see me". Those are the thoughts you need to convey. Never let this turn into a salesperson trying to get in the door. Because that, they will say "No" to.

"How long will this take?"
"I promised Bob that I would give you ten minutes. After that, if you have questions, I'll be happy to answer them. Will you be there tomorrow at 3PM?" If they ask the same question at the appointment, I say, "Do you have an appointment, or are you just curious?". If they have another appointment in 15 minutes, I'll turn it into a quick discussion about the Client (their friend) and ask if we can reschedule. Almost never does that happen. Once you are there, *and they are interested*... nobody is watching the minute hand on the clock.

"Can we talk about this right now, on the phone?"
This is a way, maybe unconsciously, to keep you away. They will listen for things to say "No" to.

"Not productively. I promised Bob that I would meet with you, and not just call you. When will you be able to squeeze in 20 minutes in the next few days? I have my appointment book out".

And if you need to... "Bob very rarely introduces people. He thinks you'll get something out of this, even if we never do business. Will you be in tomorrow around 3PM?"

"Can you just mail me the information?"
"I promised Bob to personally provide my time, to meet with you and share a couple of insights that you'll benefit from". After this, I let them get away if they want. But remember, they agreed to meet with you. You'll get this reluctance to meet you very *very* seldom.

How to force the meeting in the next couple of days.
"I'll be talking to Bob on Monday. I'd like to be able to tell him that I met with you..just like I promised him. How about tomorrow at 3PM?"

See, if they say "No" to you, they are really saying "No" to Bob, your referral source. And they already told Bob that they would talk to you. I keep making it about "me keeping my word to Bob". I know it may seem a little "Hardball" to some, but it works wonders, And I've never heard a complaint.

Sales Prospecting By Claude Whitacre

Internet Searches Before You See The Referral.
There is a very good chance that your prospect will do a search online for your company or you personally before they meet you. You have to make sure that what they find enhances your image, and makes you look in demand. A minimum of a website, a Facebook page, and a video on YouTube is needed. My book Local Online Marketing describes this entire process. But here are the essentials;

You should have a website that shows a photo of you, a short biography, and contact information. Any awards you've won, any organizations you belong to (not political). If you have client testimonials (written or on video) here's where to put them.

You can easily create a short video of you talking about the work you do, and the problems you solve. A minute is fine. Post the video on YouTube, and link it to your website.

You should have a business Facebook page. A well done Facebook page is incredibly inexpensive. Go on Fiverr.com to find a source. They can give you a good looking video too.

That's the bare bones minimum. But it's a very inexpensive way to build trust in prospects. Literally every day, I get calls from prospects who say, "I watched your video. You are the guy to help me with this". And, usually, they are right.

When A Referral Counts As A Referral.
To me, a referral doesn't count until the client has talked to the referral, and paved the way for me. The prospect is expecting my call. Until then, it's just a name on a piece of paper.

E-Mail Introductions;
Let me start by saying that I've never done this. I've had clients and students tell me that they have used e-mail introductions. For me? The phone is always better.

And I believe that the reason that someone uses e-mail introductions, is that they are simply afraid to ask for a phone introduction.

The good news is that e-mail introductions are a little easier to get than phone introductions. The bad news is that it's easy for the prospect to ignore the e-mail...or just never get it. Only use email introductions if a phone introduction is not possible. But 95% of the time, a phone introduction is possible.

Sales Prospecting By Claude Whitacre

I want the prospect to hear the source's voice, and then I want them to hear my voice. It's better than them saying, "Just tell Bob I said to give him a call", but not by much. You can easily adapt these E-Mail introductions to any offer.

These introductions are e-mailed to your client, and then he e-mails them to his referrals, with a copy to you. These are not forwarded. They are copied and pasted. The referral would then include the prospects name, in the greeting.

"I want you to meet with Claude Whitacre. Claude has been working with us to increase our leads and sales from online sources. He may be a good resource for you. So far, I've traced four sales, totaling $3,800 to his efforts, and it's been less than a month. Call me if you like.".

"I want you to meet Claude Whitacre. He has shown me how to substantially increase my sales online, and the information he gave me was worth the time spent with him. I don't know if this is a perfect fit with you, but you should talk to him, at least. Call me if you like"

"I want you to meet with Claude Whitacre. He knows a lot about boosting sales by using online marketing for your local business. He'll fill you in. Call me if you like"

I really want the referral to call my client. That will pre-sell me to the referral, or he won't see me. Either way, I won't be wasting my time. This isn't as good as the client calling the referral, but it's better than no conversation between the client and referral. Notice I didn't say, "E-Mail me if you like". Nope, it's, "Call me if you like". I want it to be a phone call.

Personal introductions are best, followed closely by a phone introduction, and then an e-mail introduction. An e-mail introduction may be better than no introduction, but not by much.

Again, I've never used (at the time of this writing) E-mail introductions. These are ideas that may make it more profitable. I strongly suggest you stick to the phone.

Researching Your Prospects;
If I'm going to see a business owner, I'll do a quick Google search for his business. It will give me a fair idea of the kind of business person they are, and how they show up online. Because I sell local online marketing programs, it also lets me know what kind of marketing they do.

I don't do the search until I have an appointment.

Sales Prospecting By Claude Whitacre

Voicemail to leave for the prospect

Even if the client has called the referral, and paved the way for you, sometimes it's just hard to get the referral on the phone. After a couple of tries, I'll resort to leaving a voicemail message.

To be completely clear, I didn't do this for years. It was either a phone conversation, or I would give up. The few times I left voicemail messages, they didn't call me back. And then I found out that I was doing it all wrong.

It's seldom that I take something directly out of a sales book, and use it as is. But I read this in the book **Beyond Referrals** by Bill Cates, and I immediately started using it with great results.

I never used to leave voice mail messages, because they would rarely call me back. But here's what I leave now on voicemail;

"Bob; This is Claude Whitacre with Local Profit Geyser. Jeff Jones told me to give you a call. I have to say, you have a real admirer in Paul. *He said some pretty nice things about you. Tell you what, I'll fill you in on what he said when we speak*" (And I give my number)

I get about 35% calling me back in a day or so. I use it as a last resort.

If you have no personal introduction.

On occasion, you'll get clients that will give you names, but won't introduce you. Whether you accept these referrals, is up to you. This can literally be used as a voicemail message, and e-mail, or even a phone call.

"Hi. Bob strongly suggested I talk to you about the work I've been doing with him for the last month or so. I don't normally do this, but Bob has asked me to spend 20 minutes with you personally, with the idea that within that time we'll be able to see if what I've been doing for him, would apply to you. Bob insisted I call you. He doesn't ask me to contact his friends without reason, and in the very few instances that he's asked me to contact someone...it's always been a beneficial meeting. Do you have 20 minutes sometime tomorrow? Call Bob, if you like. I'll call you tomorrow to set up a time."

I should say right now, that I don't contact referrals without an introduction anymore. The introductions are easy enough to get, and they keep me busy. But if you find yourself with referrals, without a personal introduction, this script will work, if anything will. It has to be constructed as *you promising Bob that you will meet with the referral. And Bob expects the referral to see you. And you have to let Bob know how it went.*

The above dialog was partly adapted from what I read in Alan Weiss's excellent book Million Dollar Referrals. I highly recommend it. I adapted his dialog, and found the ideas worked quite well.

Referrals from non-clients
By creating powerful word of mouth, you'll get referrals from people who have never done business with you. They just like to appear, "In the know". They like to recommend others based on what someone else said, or based on what they read about you online. If you find out who referred you, always thank them. There are more referrals where that came from.

Guarantee an avalanche of qualified referrals
If you are thought of as an authority, by being quoted, interviewed, or being an author, or celebrity...referrals are far easier to get, and will come to you without asking. Because people just want others to know that they *know you*.

Thanking Referrals And The Referrer Client
Thank the client for the introduction, not the result. A small token gift is appropriate. But it should be a real gift, not something promised in exchange for referrals.

Always ask the new client to thank the referral source. "When you see Bob next time could you thank him for bringing us together? He needs to know he did a good thing." You can even suggest that they send an e-mail to the referrer.

Send a thank you note, to your client, at the very least. And always let your client know how the meeting went. And no matter how it went, thank him for the introduction.

When you get a referral that buys from you
"Bob, Thank you so much for referring me to Doug Jones. We were able to get together on a project, and it was possible because of your introduction. I can't thank you enough. I'll keep you posted on the next referral I see. Take care".

When the referral is qualified, but doesn't buy
"Bob, Thank you so much for introducing me to Doug Jones. We had a productive meeting, and I think we both learned from it. We were not able to get together on a project, but he was still a great referral. I'll keep you posted on the next referral I see. Take care".

If you get unqualified referrals that don't buy
"Thank you so much for the referrals. I think you did a real favor for your friend. I should have explained who can really benefit most from meeting me. Who do you know that... (main client profile)"

"You can't build a reputation on that you are *going to do*"

-Henry Ford

www.ClaudeWhitacre.com

Past Customers... Your Untapped Vein Of Gold

The single most valuable asset you have in your business is the list of happy customers that you have served. Your customers are your most treasured resource. They will buy from you, easier than any other customer. They are already used to giving you money. They already like and trust you. And they are the best source for referrals.

Sales Prospecting By Claude Whitacre

There are three ways to sell to your customer base;

1) You can sell them a new model of what they have.

2) You can sell them more of what they have.

3) You can sell them something different.

You can sell them a new model of what they have.

Do you sell a *thing*? I sold vacuum cleaners. They were built to last a lifetime. Occasionally, I would get an appointment with someone that bought from me maybe 10 years before. I wouldn't remember the name, until I met them. And almost without fail, they already had a new vacuum cleaner. Many times, it was one that was sold through an in-home demonstration.

Eventually, it dawned on me that people were simply going to keep buying a new vacuum cleaner every so many years (I figured it out to be every 6 years, on average). So, I started keeping records, and then saw the same people every 6 or 8 years. This only works if you are going to stay in the same business for a long time. Nearly everyone I called would let me show them the new model, and nearly every one of them bought the new model from me. Who knows how many hundreds of thousands of dollars I lost by not thinking of that idea sooner?

You can sell them *more* of what they have.
If you sell a service, like life insurance, you won't be replacing the policy every few years with a new one, at least not ethically. But they can buy more from you. You can always come up with a reason to buy more of what you sell. Different applications, better results....you just have to be selling with the customer's best interests at heart. I have a friend who sells life insurance, who has maybe 500 clients. For the last 20 years, he tells me that he never cold calls, and almost never prospects for new business. His sales are nearly all to past clients, and their growing children....and an occasional referral. Now, it took him many years to build that solid base of 500 clients. But it was worth it. He essentially works six months a year, and enjoys a low six figure income.

You can sell them something different.
What if you sell several offers in different categories? What if you change companies and products? You can go back to your customers and sell them your new thing, or your new service. What you have already built up is a list of people that like you, trust you, will take your call, will see you, and have proven that they will buy from you. What more could you ask for?

Sales Prospecting By Claude Whitacre

So you want to take very good care of your customers. They will give you referrals that will likely buy from you..and they will very likely buy from you again, and again.

Company Orphans

If your company has other reps in your area, and the rep quits or leaves for any reason...what happens to those customers? Fortunes are made by taking over an absent salesperson's list of customers. Calling that list will prove very profitable. Sure, you may hear a few problems, or hear some stories about the other rep, but you will also have a group of people that are used to giving money to *someone* from your company. The other rep likely didn't ask for referrals. After you make the calls, and satisfy any complaints, you now get the repeat business and the referrals. Everyone eventually quits a job or retires. Every business eventually closes.

That customer list, is the most important part of the business, unless the business just destroyed all the customer relationships. I once bought a customer list for a product I sold for $1 a name (with all the contact information). It was a list of 5,000 names. Man, I made a profit on that list after talking to the first 100 names. I just called every name and said I was the one who was going to be providing service.

Some bought new product, some bought parts, some paid for service. And, nearly all would see me, and most bought something.

Because I see so many referrals and past customers, I no longer really look for these customer lists. But they are out there and they are worth money. If you read about anyone in your business quitting or going out of business...call them, and make them an offer for their customer files. I've had a couple sales reps just give them to me for free just so they wouldn't have to continue taking the service calls.

"It's not the mountain we conquer, but ourselves"

-Sir Edmond Hillary

Follow The Salesman

After selling vacuum cleaners for several years, a young man came to me with a problem. He had just started with the company and said, "I hear you're the company's best salesman. I need to make some real money and quick".

After listening to his story I said, "OK, I can get you several quick and easy sales.". This is before I ever started seeing my old customers. I would just sell a vacuum cleaner and move on. I didn't even ask for referrals at that time. It was all just cold calling. This is over 30 years ago.

Sales Prospecting By Claude Whitacre

So I said, "I'm going to show you where 5 very nice people live. They bought a vacuum cleaner from me about six or seven years ago, and will be happy to see the new model. Just knock on their door, tell them that you are from the company, and you are supposed to keep them updated on the new model. Believe me, some will buy".

Why I didn't do this myself, is anyone's guess. I was much younger then, and hadn't realized that seeing the same people every several years, is a very easy way to create a flood of new sales.

Anyway, my young apprentice knocked on five doors, and sold five new vacuum cleaners.

This would make a better story, if I told you that this was an, "AHA", moment for me, and I started seeing my old customers. But I was a slow study. This young salesman was literally playing, what I call "Follow the Salesman". And I started him on it. But it took a few more years for this idea of "Following the salesman" to take hold of me and change the way I prospected.

Read this next story carefully. In it, is a way to make a fortune.

I was in a home selling a vacuum cleaner. I just started asking for referrals a few months before. For some reason it came up in conversation that the prospect had bought a water softener for $5,000, maybe a year before that. My vacuum cleaner, at the time, may have been $1,000.

So I was writing up the sale and asking for referrals.

One of the people said, "Do you just want us to give you the names that we gave the water softener guy?". Something about that question made neurons in my brain fire in the right way.

I said, "Yes. Do you know who the buyers were? In other words, which of the referrals, you gave the water softener guy, bought a water softener from him?"

And they *did* know who bought, and they gave me *those* names.

And from that point on, when seeing someone in this referral chain, I only asked for referral names of the people who already bought a water softener, from this other salesman. Every one of these leads bought from me. And nearly every one of these leads gave me referrals of people who bought from the water softener guy. This one list of referrals kept me busy, every day...for months.

Sales Prospecting By Claude Whitacre

And all of them were buying. It couldn't have been easier, or more profitable.

Here is why this idea was so incredibly profitable. See how you can apply this to what you sell.

I was selling in people's homes. Here are some educated guesses about how that works.

Most people will not let a salesperson into their home. I'm one of them. Never. Under any circumstances. And the better the home, the higher the income...the harder it is to see that person in their home. Maybe 80% of the homeowners will simply not let you in their home.

Of the people that will let you in their home, only a third will buy whatever you sell. That seems to be pretty average for every sales organization I've talked to. One out of three will buy.

Of the people who buy only some will give you referrals and introduce you to them. When I first discovered the "Follow the Salesman" method, I was not very adept at getting referrals...like most people in sales. But let's say that half will give you a short list of referrals.

My math gives me the educated guess, that only six percent of the homeowners out there will buy from an in-home salesperson.

That's still enough to make a good living. But....

What if you changed that six percent to ninety five percent? What if you were now *only* talking to that six percent that are *used to buying from an in-home salesperson*?

Your income would shoot through the roof, and mine did.

Remember the 80/20 rule? Well, using this "Follow the Salesman" method, I was using the 94/6 Rule. I was only seeing the best 6% of the population. Spending 100% of my time only with proven buyers.

Another reason this worked was that I was selling something that cost less than what the other salesperson was selling. I don't know if I would get the same results, if I were selling the $5,000 offer, and he had sold the $1,000 offer. I just don't know.

But I was only seeing people that were used to buying from an in-home salesperson, and they were used to giving referrals to that salesperson. And I was only seeing the buyers.

The one problem with this system, is that I was seeing the referrals faster than my unknown "partner" was seeing his prospects.

Sales Prospecting By Claude Whitacre

You see, I was only seeing his buyers. And he was seeing everyone that he presented to. So he was moving through his prospects much slower than I was moving through his buyers.

So I had to find other salespeople, that I could "follow". I had a life insurance salesman, an encyclopedia salesman, and several vacuum cleaner salespeople that sold a different brand.

Now that you have read this far into my book, I want to let you in on a little secret. This "Follow the Salesman" idea is the single most profitable system I have ever used. It is the main system that I was using, when I broke my many sales records.

But beware. Do not do the reverse. Do not tell other salespeople, in other businesses, about this idea. They will never think of it on their own, and it has a cost. Here it is...

Warning!
If you give a salesperson friend the names of a few people you sold years ago, and tell them about this program, you will eventually have a problem. After the salesperson runs all the referrals that bought from you, they will catch up to you. And then they will sell past you.

I once gave a friend of mine, in the insurance business, a name of one of my customers that bought years before. Being the enterprising guy that he was, he also got referrals from that customer...the referrals that bought from me. Are you starting to guess the rest of the story?

He had a great month or two, and I was glad to help. But then, I went on an appointment in the same referral tree and they said, "We would love to buy from you, but we just took out a large life insurance policy from Dave. He says you and he are friends."

And no, the sale was not made, and I didn't get the referrals that my friend Dave got.

I didn't think anything badly about my friend. He was doing his job. But I realized that eventually, the salesperson will get ahead of you, and may muddy the waters for you, when you start seeing *his* clients...the clients that could have been yours.

"Give a man a fish, you feed him for a day. Teach a man to fish, you feed him for a lifetime. Sell a man fish every day, and you have a nice little business"

-Claude

What Do They Buy *Before* They Buy *Your* Product/Service?

I don't know what you sell. But this will probably apply to what you sell, if you just think about it. I honestly don't remember when I learned this, or figured it out on my own. But it's a powerful question to ask yourself.

What is something that people tend to buy before they buy your offer?

Sales Prospecting By Claude Whitacre

I can give you real life examples from my businesses.

When I was selling vacuum cleaners in people's homes I noticed that the people who had just bought new carpet were easier to sell than people with older carpet, or bare floors. Why?

Because they had invested more in their carpet than in my vacuum cleaner. And my vacuum cleaner would protect their investment in new carpet. The new vacuum cleaner would get rid of the sand and grit that cut carpet fibers, when you walked on the carpet. Also, it kept the carpet fibers standing straight up, making the carpet look nicer.

Soooo

I went to a few of the larger carpet dealers, and asked them for the names of the people that had bought carpet in the last few months. Why would they give me those names? First, because I was bragging up the quality of the carpet they bought, and word got back to the dealers, and they wanted me to see more of their customers to help promote their stores. The other reason was that I gave each store a free vacuum cleaner, and free service.

I didn't tell customers that I was from the carpet store, or that we had anything to do with each other.

I tell you now, it would have been smarter to make that arrangement.

But I was calling people that I *knew* had new, high quality carpet in their home. I also knew that they could afford my new vacuum cleaner, or at least qualify for financing. And it was such a natural thing to say to them, "You just bought new carpet for your home. If you were ever going to take care of it, and keep it clean, when would be the best time to start?"

And usually, they would say, "As soon as possible". It was a natural sale, and my closing percentage on these sales was better than 80%. And that was essentially a cold call.

I knew that these leads were already super qualified, and they already had a reason to buy from me. So I gave a great gift for letting me show them my vacuum cleaner. It wasn't for buying, just taking a look.

When I'm selling my local online marketing service to brick and mortar businesses, I also think, "What do they buy before they buy my thing?"

And you know what it is? Print and broadcast advertising. The business owners who buy lots of local radio, cable TV, and print advertising are *far* more likely to buy my online marketing service.

Sales Prospecting By Claude Whitacre

Why?

Because they're used to buying lots of advertising. And every ad that they run, can point to my online marketing. Their newspaper ad can direct the customer to a website I built for the business. The people seeing the ads can be directed to videos I produce for the business. It all fits together nicely. I don't give gifts for these appointments. But when I get a newspaper in the mail, or a direct mail ad from a merchant...They are getting a call from me.

The approach I use?

"Hi, Bob? This is Claude Whitacre. I help mattress stores with their advertising. I'm looking at your ad right now for mattresses. It's a fine ad. But it's missing two things that could make it at least twice as profitable. Would you like to know how to do that? (Yes). Good. I create quality leads and sales for businesses that already advertise in the newspaper (or wherever I saw the ad). I'll show you how to make your current advertising less expensive and far more productive. All I ask is that you'll keep me in mind, if you ever need any of my online services. Fair enough? (Sure, I guess. Can you tell me now?)

Bob, I want to meet with you for a moment, to show you the ad, and point out how to make it more profitable. Will you be in tomorrow between 2 and 3PM?".

And one out of three times, maybe a tad more, they say "Yes" to the appointment. And almost always, they buy my service. Why? Because they are already buying just about every other thing that advertises for them. Want to sell fish? Find someone who eats a ton of fish. Stop trying to convince a vegetarian to eat fish.

Now, here is your exercise for today; Think of at least two things people buy, that makes them more likely to buy *your* product. It should be something that costs more than your product, to make your sale easier.

"The key to a good elevator talk, is that it's short, sounds like something a human being would actually say, and causes the right people to ask 'how do you do that?'"

-Claude

Your Elevator Speech

Your Real Elevator Talk.
In every book on selling and marketing there is a section on your "Positioning statement" or your "Elevator talk". In several seminars I've attended the speaker takes us through an exercise… and we all give our "Elevator talk". It begins with you asking someone what they do for a living, and they tell you. Then they are asked what you do for a living. Big Mistake! Because they might hear something someone learned at one of these seminars.

Sales Prospecting By Claude Whitacre

They all sound something like this; Someone says, "What do you do for a living?"

"I help companies maximize revenue share while accentuating efficiency in multiple departments by vertical integration". I'm not joking, they almost all sound like that. They all sound like something you would never say in a real conversation.

After you try your new "Elevator talk" a few times, and people look at you like you are crazy, you stop using it. When I hear speakers talk about these long convoluted "elevator talks", I promise you this...they aren't using it themselves. They got it out of a book that was written by someone who *also* didn't use it themselves.

When someone asks what you do, do not say;

"I work for a major conglomerate that lowers your fuel bills, while providing world class service". It's better, but it still doesn't sound like anything a human being would say. And it tells the person nothing about what you offer.

Don't say, "I'm working for a wonderful company that makes wonderful products that will cure whatever ails you. And you can put it on your credit card". See? No human being would talk like that. Although I've heard worse at some of these "Create your elevator talk" seminars.

Don't say, "I am the chief marketing account executive at a major conglomerate, that builds private equity for discerning investors" If you say that, and the person says "Huh?", that's not a good response.

When someone ask you what you do, they want to hear you say; "Doctor, pizza delivery guy, construction worker, police officer, hotel manager"..that sort of thing. If you go on and on, trying to be impressive, it's falling on deaf ears.

You just want to say a benefit that you deliver. Make it quick. Then give a qualification that makes you sound selective. It must sound like you are very matter of fact. There can be no enthusiasm, no selling. I say it like I would say, "Would you pass the salt?"

Here's mine. Someone says, "What do you do?"

"I create quality leads and sales for businesses, that already have a website". And then I shut up.

They either say, "That's nice" or they ask, "How do you do that?" If the later, I say

"Do you own a business that people can find online?" (Yes)

"Do you ever have customers tell you that they found you online?" (Yes)

Sales Prospecting By Claude Whitacre

"Would you like more of them?" (Yeah, I sure would)

"Well, I'm not sure we're a perfect match, but we can find out in a few minutes. Do you have a card?".....and we get off the elevator. Am I telling you that I've said exactly that, on an elevator, and they went on to be a client? Yes, that's what I'm telling you. And I say the same thing at trade shows, community meetings, and business mixers.

At no time, if they don't ask you, "how do you do that?" or, "how does that work?" do you ask to talk further. You either just stop talking, or change the subject. For example;

'"What do you do for a living?"

"I create quality leads and sales for businesses that already have a website. What time is it?"

I want them to say, "Wait. Why do they need a website to talk to you?" or, "How do you get them sales?". I want them to chase me a little.

Years ago, when I was selling vacuum cleaners in people's homes I would get asked, "What do you do?"

For several years, I would just say, "I'm in sales". But that didn't tell them anything.

Eventually, I decided to start saying, "I sell quality vacuum cleaners, by appointment only".

And usually, they would say, "That's nice, do you know what time it is?". But about once every 100 times, I told that to someone, they would say, "Really? We're looking for a good vacuum cleaner. Tell me about yours". And I've sold maybe a dozen expensive vacuums every year just by changing how I answer, "What do you do for a living?"

How to craft the perfect "elevator talk"
First, be very brief. Ten seconds maybe. The first half is what your customers want. The second half is a "conversational limitation".

So the elevator talk is; (Result my clients want) and then (A limitation that spurs conversation)

Remember? "I create quality leads and sales, *for businesses that already have a website*"

And then they may ask, "Why do we need to already have a website?" and I say, "Are you the owner of the company?" (Yes), "Do you have a website?" (Yes), "Would you like everyone going on line to be able to find it?" (Yes)

"Maybe we should talk. Do you have a card? I'll call you in a few days to ask a few more questions to see if we are a match. OK?"

Sales Prospecting By Claude Whitacre

I use the same thing at conferences, local mixers, and yes, elevators.

This is almost the same thing I say when I'm cold calling someone on the phone.

Here are several other ways to give a good "elevator talk"

"I show people how to...." or, "I show *veterinarians* how to...."

If you have a product or service that you only sell to one occupation, I would include it here.

For example, you sell only to hospital nursing staff. You might say, "I show hospital nurses how to...", and then you just give a benefit. That way if the person asking isn't in your market they will just keep talking, but not with any intention of doing business with you. It's an invisible technique. Nobody can reject you, because you aren't asking anyone for anything.

For example, "I show people how to lose weight, without getting hungry".

If you are talking to a woman you might say, "I show *women* how to lose weight, without getting hungry". See? Now it's more specific to the person asking you the question.

They are now more likely to ask you more about it. But again, don't volunteer any more information about what you do. They have to *ask*. You are simply leaving openings for someone to ask. Never prompt them in any way.

One more.

"Well, you know how ... (problem)" "Well, what I do is ... (benefit)"

For example, "Well, you know how your widows leak heat in the winter?" (Yes), "Well, what I do is show people how to seal their windows, and save money on electricity. Have you seen where the coffee pot is?"

This last one was a little more involved. You are asking them to verify a problem, and then you are giving a solution. It's more likely now that the person will ask you a question. They are slightly more involved. But you still either stop talking or change the subject. You have to be completely nonchalant about it. Never say, "Well, you know how weeds grow in your yard all Summer?" (Yeah), "Well, what I do is take care of lawns so that doesn't happen. Can I give you a quote?"

"Can I give you a quote?" is too invasive. It's too abrupt. You'll get people avoiding you.

Sales Prospecting By Claude Whitacre

Just say, "Well, what I do is take care of lawns so that doesn't happen. Have you seen the napkins?" If there is any interest at all, they will let you know.

A good elevator talk is impossible to say "No" to. That doesn't mean everyone will ask you for more information, but it takes out the "Rejection factor". You're simply leaving an opening, where the person can ask you a question, if your talk resonates with them.

For people that your quick talk doesn't apply, or if they not interested, they will simply keep the conversation going in the same direction as before.

How to increase the chance that they will ask about your business.

If you ask the person what they do for a living, and they don't immediately ask what you do for a living, ask them a second question about their business. I always ask them something that either helps qualify them as a good prospect, or disqualifies them. Either way, it gives them another chance to ask about my business. For example;

"Is that a brick and mortar business, or do you work out of your home?"

"What kind of marketing do you do to promote your business?"

"Do you do the marketing yourself, or do you farm it out to suppliers?"

I'll just ask one additional question after, "What kind of work do you do?". I don't want to spend 30 minutes talking about why his cardboard boxes are better than everyone else's cardboard boxes. Sometimes these people are actually interesting, and you will engage in a real conversation. Sometimes, I get interested in their business, just because it's interesting, not because they would make a great prospect. But I keep reminding myself that I'm prospecting, not engaging in small talk...no matter what it looks like.

Where to give your short "Elevator talk"
Do you attend conferences? Trade shows? Networking meetings? Business group meetings?

When I attend a trade show, where the attendees fit my client profiles, I'm there to prospect.

Usually, there are speakers. If I'm not going to speak, I walk around at the breaks. This is when I'm actually working. I don't interrupt small huddles of people talking. I look for the guy standing by himself, trying to look like he wants to be there. I just walk over and ask, "So, what brings you here?"

Sales Prospecting By Claude Whitacre

The next question is, "What do you do for a living?"

If he doesn't ask me what I do for a living, I just say a few pleasant things and move on.

If he asks what I do for a living, I give my short talk, and see what his response is. I easily let it go if there is no question on his part. They never even perceive that I'm asking for any reason other than to be nice.

I never offer my card. I always ask for their card. But I don't ask unless there is real interest. I immediately note on the back of their card, what I'm calling them about, and any other information I think I could use. Then I put these "really call them" cards in one pocket. The cards that I won't call, go in a different pocket. If someone says, "Hi, I build birdbaths. Here's my card", that's the pocket that card goes into.

Personally, I won't go to an event just to do this networking. I may have a few thousand dollars in plane tickets, hotel room, and meals. But if I'm attending anyway? I usually end up with two to five new clients on every trip.

A side note. If you go to an event where there are a thousand attendees, usually ten percent or more, are there mainly for the networking.

I have a good friend that does marketing for dentists. He attends dental conferences. Working the room, is the main way he gets his new clients... that and referrals. He attends three or four conferences a year, and that's his main prospecting method. In fact, he's the one that, several years ago, showed me the basics of working a show floor.

If you can attend a local meeting where everyone stands up and introduces themselves, you'll get a great result just saying the new short "Elevator talk" you just learned.

I say my one short sentence, and I always get one or two people at the break ask me, "What do you mean, you create qualified leads? Would that work for a tire store?" or, "I already have a website. What can you do for me?". About half the time, I get a new client out of it.

"Suffering from burn out? Nobody ever felt burned out while they were *learning*"

-Claude

Keeping Track Of It All

I'm sure that there are several programs you can use to keep track of your cold call, referrals, and contacts. Me? I use a form that I just print out whenever I need them.

For cold calling.
I just use half a sheet of typing paper that includes the following information;

- The time I started on the phone
- The time I stopped
- How many contacts
- How many appointments

Sales Prospecting By Claude Whitacre

At the top, I write where I got the list. To keep tabs of the number of calls I just use a "1", an then cross off every bundle of five. This way, I can tell how my cold calling is going per hour.

I don't track my cold calls all the way through to how many buy. But it isn't a bad idea.

If you use the Callfire.com dialing software, it will keep these records for you.

What you will find is that you are making several appointments in a two hour cold calling session. But you can't cheat. I don't count people I've called a second time. Playing "telephone tag" doesn't help. Every new number called, is a call. I only start counting when I'm talking to a business owner. You may also want to include "Dials". If you call at different times of the day, you'll eventually see when the most productive time is to call. For me, it's usually before 10AM.

For Referrals from Clients

It's a printed sheet. One page per client. I have room for 8 referrals, and the space to keep some notes. I use it on the phone, and also in front of clients. Sometimes, I just get the names on a legal pad and then transfer the information over. I keep a small stack of these referral lists, when I 'm calling. But when we have all the results, the sheet just goes into the client file.

Depending on what you sell your gathered information will be different. But here is what my sheet asks for each name. At the top, is the name of the client, his phone number, and the date I got the names

Each name has the following spaces;

- The referral's name.
- How the client knows the referral
- Referral's business name, and what kind of business it is. How long in business.
- Partners? Names?
- Why I should see them.
- Were they ever a referral for someone else? Did they buy?
- The referral's phone number
- The referral's website, if known.
- Date talked to, Date seen, Result (sale/no sale)

At the end of the day, I'll send out the "Thank you cards" to the clients that gave me a referral that bought. I'll also send e-mails to the client, to let them know about the activity on the referral list.

Want To Know More?
Of course there is more. I gave you the very best advice I could, with the very best sales prospecting methods I've found. But there is always more to learn.

Sales Prospecting By Claude Whitacre

If you just invested in thoroughly learning one of the methods that are in this book, you could be booked solid.

But there is more to selling. Much more.

Soon, I'll have a complete selling system online that will include insights that you just can't include in a mainstream book. You'll get the best advice on every aspect of selling. All of it with the goal of closing your sales in one call.

You can go to www.onecallcloser.com if you like. I may have an offer there, I may not.

I wrote this book before I started to create this vast project. It may not be done when you get there.

May I suggest that you also check out my book on closing, **One Call Closing**?

And if you really liked what you read in this book, I would be honored if you would leave a review on Amazon. Other readers read your reviews . They are looking for advice on what they should read. They could use your help.

www.ClaudeWhitacre.com

"Selling is not something we do *to* people, it's something we do *with* people, and *for* them"

-Claude

Recommended Reading

I want to be clear. Everyone learns how to prospect from somewhere. For me, much of my referral prospecting was learned decades ago in the field. The same with cold calling. But, I read books to get better perspectives on what works. This is a learning process. Some of the dialog I use in sales prospecting has been improved by what I've read in these books. All of these books are in my "Prospecting Library", and I recommend them all. Every once in a while, I'll thumb through my copy of one of these books, and say, "So *that's* where I picked that idea up!".

Use a yellow highlighter. You'll need one.

High Probability Selling by Jacques Werth and Nicholas E. Ruben. This book opened my eyes to selling by cold calling over the phone, and turning every calling into a sorting, rather than selling process. Highly recommended.

Endless Referrals by Bob Burg. This book is where I learned about many of the other books on prospecting with referrals.. Lots of resources in the book. Great overview of the networking process.

Sales Prospecting By Claude Whitacre

Get More Referrals Now by Bill Cates. The first Bill Cates book I ever read, and a real treasure on getting referrals.

Beyond Referrals: How to Use the Perpetual Revenue System to Convert Referrals into High-Value Clients by Bill Cates. This book gives solid methodologies on using introductions with your referrals. This book changed the way I ask for referrals.

Don't Keep Me A Secret: Proven Tactics to Get Referrals and Introductions by Bill Cates.

These three books explain, in complete detail, how to get referrals and use networking to help build your business. This book, is more the type of book you present to a client as a gift, or use to prospect for clients. There is a lot of "What to do", but not much "How to do it". Cate's book Beyond Referrals gives most of the real meat.

Smart Calling: Eliminate the Fear, Failure, and Rejection from Cold Calling by Art Sobczak. Lots of scripts, tips, and strategies for selling on the phone. A softer approach than what I use. I can see where this approach would be preferred by many salespeople. If you have a much shorter list of prospects to call, this is a great approach to cold calling. A solid book with solid advice.

How To Master The Art Of Selling by Tom Hopkins My first book on selling that changed what I was doing. A real eye opener, when I was selling in the early 1980's.

Red Hot Introductions by Randy Schwantz. This short little book is where I learned the difference between a referral and an introduction, many years ago. This is a book about selling insurance, but I find the best ideas in books about businesses outside my own.

You Can't Teach a Kid to Ride a Bike at a Seminar by David Sandler. A few years ago, a friend told me that I had to buy this book. I asked why, and he said "You'll see". This selling system nearly mirrors my own. Sandler arrived at the same conclusions from a completely different path. But it's a revealing read.

The Referral Engine by John Jantsch. A different approach to using referral marketing.

Million Dollar Referrals by Alan Weiss. I primarily read Weiss's books on speaking and consulting. But his book on referrals showed deep insights and helped sculpt the way I talked to referrals. A must read, if prospecting for new sales.

Sales Prospecting By Claude Whitacre

Cold Calling Techniques That Really Work by Stephen Schiffman. You need to get the completely rewritten 2014 edition. This book actually changed the way I answered objections when cold calling. This book was written by someone who uses what he teaches. I can't recommend this book highly enough.

There are two other approaches for cold calling on the phone. I don't use them but I'll address them here, because you'll eventually think of them yourself.

The Ultimate Book Of Phone Scripts by Mike Brooks. This book costs about $35 on Amazon, but it's worth every penny. If you sell anything by phone, this book will give you all the scripts that you need to get the sale.

Local Online Marketing by Claude Whitacre. The book I wrote about how to market your business online. This is a great resource to give prospects an image of you, before they see you in person. My websites, videos, and articles get seen by prospects before I see them, and it changes how they think of me. This can work for you too.

One Call Closing by Claude Whitacre. This is the book I wrote just before this one. It covers what to do once you get in front of the prospect.

www.ClaudeWhitacre.com

About The Author

Claude Whitacre has been selling to consumers, belly to belly, for 40 years. First, selling life insurance, then vacuum cleaners, then high end online marketing services to local business owners. He now divides his time between speaking to groups of business owners and salespeople about increasing their sales, and selling high end marketing services to business owners. He also owns a retail store in Wooster, Ohio, with his wife Cheryl.

Other Books by Claude Whitacre:
- *The Unfair Advantage Small Business Advertising Manual*
- *Selling Local Advertising*
- *Local Online Marketing*
- *One Call Closing*

For information about booking Claude to speak for your group, just go to: www.ClaudeWhitacre.com
Or e-mail: Claude@LocalProfitGeyser.com

Claude speaks to groups of salespeople and groups of business owners, and nobody else.

One Last Thing... If you found this book useful, I'd be very grateful if you'd post a short review on Amazon. Your support really does make a difference and I read all the reviews personally so I can get your feedback and make this book even better. If you'd like to leave a review, all you need to do is find my book on Amazon and leave your review.

Thanks again for your support!

Printed in Great Britain
by Amazon.co.uk, Ltd.,
Marston Gate.